Sunset

BEST
KIDS ™
COOK BOOK

By the Sunset Editors

Sunset Publishing Corporation ■ **Menlo Park, California**

FOREST HOUSE ™
School & Library Edition

Join the Best Kids in the Kitchen

Research & Text
Sue Brownlee

Art Direction
Susan Bryant

Coordinating Editor
Deborah Thomas Kramer

Illustration
R. W. Alley

Design
Katherine Tillotson

Photography
Tom Wyatt

Photo Styling
Susan Massey-Weil

Editor, Sunset Books: Elizabeth L. Hogan

First printing September 1992

Get ready to cook! Make main dishes, snacks, desserts, and holiday treats you'll be proud to serve to your family and share with your friends. You'll find over 50 recipes to try; let an adult cook with you, or choose a recipe marked with a star and cook on your own. We've even included plans and menus for six parties—some fancy, some just plain fun. All our recipes were tested, tasted, and approved by a panel of boys and girls ranging in age from six to 14. Begin by reading Chapter 1, "Cook Your Best"—then join the best kids in the kitchen!

We offer special thanks to Karen Ross, R.D., consulting nutritionist in Cardiovascular and Sports Nutrition and Wellness, for her contribution to the text and her assistance in food styling. Thanks also to Lynn Meaders, elementary education teacher in the Palo Alto Unified School District, for sharing her experience and time with us. Both Karen and Lynn have given us invaluable advice in the preparation and review of this book.

We thank Rebecca LaBrum for her skillful and careful editing of the manuscript. Her comments, offered with humor and patience, were greatly appreciated.

We thank Jerry Anne Di Vecchio, Senior Editor (Food and Entertaining), *Sunset* magazine, for her editorial review of the manuscript.

For each of our recipes, we provide a nutritional analysis (see pages 110 and 111) prepared by Hill Nutrition Associates, Inc., of Florida. We thank Lynne Hill, R.D., for her expertise.

Our sincere thanks go to Dave Schaub and his talented staff at Schaub's Meat, Fish & Poultry; and to Ken Fujimoto at Monterey Market. We are grateful to Fillamento, RH, Cotton Works, At the Zoo, and Williams-Sonoma for props used in our photographs.

Thank you to the children and teachers at Duveneck Elementary School in Palo Alto, California, for their participation in our research. Finally, we thank our test panel of kids: Roni Brown, Katie Conway, Maggie Goloboy, Nathan Kramer, Hilary and Lindsey Selden, Jason Stolpa, and Lance Wu.

CONTENTS

Special Features

COOK YOUR BEST

BEST
YUMMIEST
PIE

Best Beginnings

Cooking is fun! There's lots of measuring and mixing—and best of all, you get to eat what you make. To guarantee that what you cook will be delicious, be sure to start off right. Always keep the following guidelines in mind:

1 Read "Safety Pointers" (page 7) before beginning a recipe. **Remember that any recipe using a sharp utensil, an appliance, or a heat source requires adult participation.** Make sure you have permission and time to use the kitchen.

2 Read your recipe through completely. Check "Cooking Terms" (pages 8 and 9) to review new words.

3 Gather all the equipment you will need. We list every utensil required for a recipe, from measuring cups to oven mitts. Use "Cooking Equipment" (pages 10 and 11) to check new tools.

4 Make sure you have all your ingredients. We list everything in the order in which it appears in the recipe instructions. Check the introduction to each recipe for ingredient substitutions or serving ideas.

5 Follow the recipe step by step. Use "Cooking Techniques" (pages 12 and 13) to review new methods.

6 Read "Entertaining Tips" (pages 14 and 15) for table-setting suggestions.

7 Read "Good for You" (pages 16 and 17) to learn more about being your best. Look at the "Tell a friend. . ." boxes to learn useful food facts. You can also find a nutritional analysis for each of our recipes on pages 110 and 111.

8 Best beginnings deserve best endings. Don't forget to clean up the kitchen when you are finished!

TELL A FRIEND THAT. . .
any recipe with a star
may be done without
adult participation.

Safety Pointers

To avoid accidents in the kitchen, always follow these safety pointers.

1 Remember that any recipe using a sharp utensil (knife, vegetable peeler, or grater), an appliance (electric mixer, blender, or food processor), or a heat source (stovetop, oven, or waffle iron) requires adult participation.

2 Thoroughly wash your hands before and after cooking, especially after handling eggs and raw meat.

3 To prevent burns, use thick, dry oven mitts when carrying hot baking dishes and cooking pans.

4 To avoid burning or otherwise damaging countertops, set hot food on wire racks placed near oven or stovetop.

5 To prevent bumps and spills, turn pot handles away from you, toward center of stovetop.

6 Turn off oven and burners when you're not using them.

7 Pick up knives only by the handle; cut only on a cutting board. When using a vegetable peeler, move it away from, not toward, your body. When grating, hold food carefully, so you grate only the food and not your fingers.

8 Before plugging in or unplugging appliances, make sure they are turned off and that your hands are clean and dry.

9 Put a spoon or spatula in an electric mixer bowl or in a blender or processor container only when the appliance is turned off. Always keep your fingers away from appliance blades.

10 Before turning on a blender, make sure lid is securely in place.

11 Clean up any spills quickly.

Cooking Terms

If you're reading a recipe and come across a term you don't know, look here for the definition.

Bake: To cook, covered or uncovered, by dry heat.

Batter: A liquid mixture (containing flour and other ingredients) that can be dropped from a spoon or poured.

Beat: To stir or mix rapidly, adding air with a quick, even, circular motion. Beating makes a mixture smoother, lighter, and fluffier.

Blend: To combine two or more ingredients thoroughly, until the mixture is smooth and uniform in texture, color, and flavor.

Boil: To cook liquid rapidly so that bubbles constantly rise and break on the surface.

Broil: To cook by direct heat in the broiler of an electric or gas range.

Chop: To cut food into small pieces.

Core: To remove the center of a fruit or vegetable.

Dough: A thick mixture of flour and liquid, usually firm enough to be kneaded or shaped with the hands.

Flour: To sprinkle lightly with flour and shake off the excess.

Fold: To gently combine a light, delicate substance (such as beaten egg whites) with a heavier mixture, using a light over-and-under motion.

Fry: To cook in hot fat.

Grease: To rub fat or oil on the surface of a baking sheet or pan to prevent food from sticking.

Knead: To work dough with the hands in a fold-and-press motion.

Marinate: To soak in a seasoned liquid.

Boil

Knead

Punch down

Simmer

Peel: To remove skin or rind.

Pit: To remove the large central seed from a whole fruit such as a peach or plum.

Preheat: To heat the oven to the desired temperature before beginning to cook.

Punch down: To remove air from a risen yeast dough by pushing it down in the center with your fist.

Simmer: To cook in liquid over low heat just below the boiling point (bubbles form slowly and burst before reaching the surface).

Steam: To cook in water vapor, on a rack above boiling water in a covered pan.

Stir: To mix ingredients without beating, by moving a utensil (such as a spoon) through the ingredients in a broad circular motion. Cooked mixtures are often stirred to prevent the food from sticking to the pan.

Stir-fry: To cook sliced food quickly in a small amount of fat over high heat, stirring constantly.

Toss: To mix lightly and rapidly by lifting and turning ingredients with two forks or spoons.

Weights & Measures
3 teaspoons = 1 tablespoon
2 tablespoons = 1 fluid ounce
4 tablespoons = ¼ cup
5 tablespoons + 1 teaspoon = ⅓ cup
8 tablespoons = ½ cup

12 tablespoons = ¾ cup
16 tablespoons = 1 cup = 8 fluid ounces
2 cups = 16 fluid ounces = 1 pint
4 cups = 2 pints = 1 quart
4 quarts = 1 gallon
16 ounces = 1 pound

Cooking Equipment

Standard cup
for liquid measuring

Standard cups
for dry measuring

Standard
measuring spoons

Mixing bowls

Double boiler

1-, 2-, 3-quart
pans & lids

4- to 5-quart pan
(Dutch oven) & lid

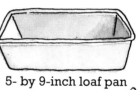

2-quart baking dish

Small frying pan

Large frying pan & lid

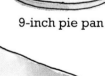

9-inch-square
baking pan

9- by 13-inch
baking pan

5- by 9-inch loaf pan

9-inch pie pan

9-inch-round
baking pan

12- by 15-inch
baking sheet

10- by 15-inch baking pan

Muffin pan

14-inch pizza pan

10

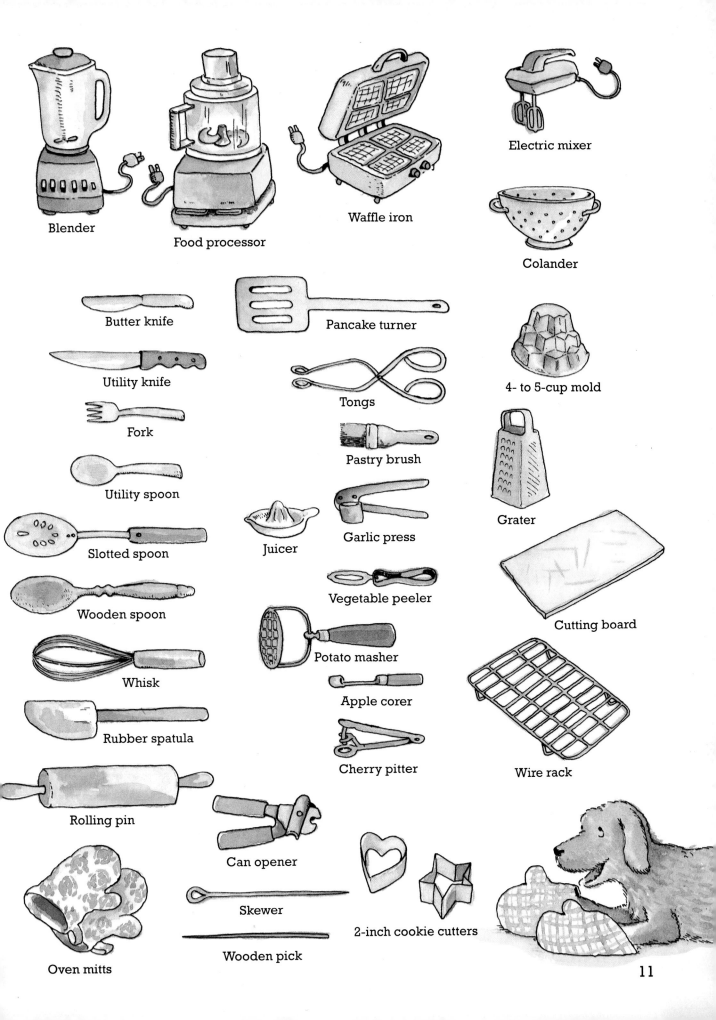

Blender

Food processor

Waffle iron

Electric mixer

Colander

Butter knife

Pancake turner

4- to 5-cup mold

Utility knife

Tongs

Fork

Pastry brush

Grater

Utility spoon

Juicer

Garlic press

Slotted spoon

Vegetable peeler

Cutting board

Wooden spoon

Potato masher

Whisk

Apple corer

Rubber spatula

Cherry pitter

Wire rack

Rolling pin

Can opener

Oven mitts

Skewer

Wooden pick

2-inch cookie cutters

11

Cooking Techniques

For best results from any recipe, use proper cooking methods. Described here are 12 techniques called for in this book.

1 **To measure liquid ingredients:** Place glass cup on level surface, pour in ingredient, and read markings on cup at eye level.

2 **To measure dry ingredients:** Scoop metal or plastic cup (or measuring spoon) into ingredient, piling high; then level off with butter knife.

3 **To measure brown sugar:** Use fingers to pack sugar firmly into metal or plastic cup until sugar is even with rim.

4 **To measure margarine or butter:** Place 8-tablespoon stick on cutting board and use butter knife to cut off desired amount.

5 **To measure shredded cheese:** Lightly pile shreds, without packing, in metal or plastic cup until even with rim.

6 **To chop an onion:** Hold knife by "shaking hands" with handle. Cut stem end off onion on cutting board. Peel off outer skin. Cut onion in half lengthwise; place halves, cut side down, on board. Cut onion halves lengthwise into thin strips, taking care not to cut to root end of onion. Then cut onion halves crosswise into small chunks. Discard root end.

7 **To grate peel from a lemon or orange:** Carefully rub fruit against sharp holes of grater to shred off colored part of peel only.

8 **To crack an egg:** Gently tap egg on counter and use your fingers to pull shell apart at crack, dropping egg into bowl.

9 **To separate an egg:** Crack egg, pull shell apart, and carefully drop egg into a small bowl, being sure not to break yolk. Then pour egg from bowl into your hand; open your fingers to let white fall into a clean container. Drop yolk back into bowl.

10 **To fold:** Use sharp edge of a rubber spatula to cut straight down center of mixture to bottom; turn spatula as if scraping side of bowl and bring spatula up

out of mixture with straight side up. Meanwhile, use your other hand to turn bowl slightly. Repeat until mixture is blended.

11 **To grease and flour baking pans:** Use your fingers to lightly spread margarine, butter, or oil on bottom and sides of pan. Sprinkle some flour into pan and shake pan, tilting it slightly, to cover bottom and sides. Turn pan upside down over sink and tap lightly to remove excess flour.

12 **To remove cake from pan and turn right side up:** Let cake cool for about 10 minutes in pan. Run butter knife between edge of cake and pan. Place rack over pan and, holding rack and pan with oven mitts, turn upside down. Remove pan. Place another rack over cake and, holding both racks, turn upside down again; then remove top rack.

Entertaining Tips

It's easy to transfer your talents from kitchen to table—just use a little basic setting sense!

1 Place dinner plates about 1 inch from edge of table.

2 Place knife to right of plate, with bottom of knife handle level with bottom edge of plate. Make sure cutting edge of knife faces plate.

3 Place spoons to right of knife. Arrange them in the order they'll be used, with spoon to be used first farthest away from plate.

4 Place forks to left of plate, level with knife. Arrange them in the order they'll be used, with fork to be used first farthest away from plate.

5 Dessert utensils can be placed horizontally above the dinner plate. Place glasses above knife to right of dinner plate.

6 Bread-and-butter and salad plates go to left of dinner plate, above forks and level with glasses.

7 You can place the napkin almost anywhere: to left of fork, on dinner plate, or tucked into a glass.

8 To fold a napkin in a simple way, first fold it in half, making a rectangle with fold at top; then fold rectangle in half again to make a square, with open edges meeting on left and at bottom. Finally, fold napkin in half again; then place it on table, with fold near plate and loose edges at lower left.

9 To fold a napkin in a fancy way, see drawings 1 through 6 at left and below. First, fold napkin in half to make a rectangle, with fold on right and open edges at left. Starting with short edge closest to you, crease napkin in 1-inch accordion pleats. Pleat to within about 4 inches of top edge. Fold napkin in half by turning right half of rectangle underneath. Pleats should be outside and at bottom; folded edge should be at right. Turn down upper left corner and tuck it behind last pleat. Holding tucked-in corner in one hand, place that corner on table; center of fold should be on table, with pleats on either side. Spread pleats into a fan shape. Tucked-in corner acts as a stand at back to hold open fan upright.

10 To serve the meal, pass plates from left of seated person and remove them from the right, the same way food is passed at the table. (Salad and bread-and-butter plates are an exception; they're removed from the left, because they're on that side.)

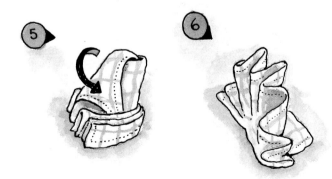

Good for You

Be your best by practicing good eating habits. Nutrients found in food—carbohydrates, protein, fat, vitamins, and minerals—are body builders. They give you energy, help you grow, and support good health.

1 To get all the nutrients you need, eat a variety of foods from five basic food groups: bread, cereals, rice, and pasta; vegetables; fruits; milk, yogurt, and cheese; and meat, poultry, fish, dry beans, eggs, and nuts. No one food meets all your body's daily requirements.

Food Guide Pyramid
A Guide to Daily Food Choices

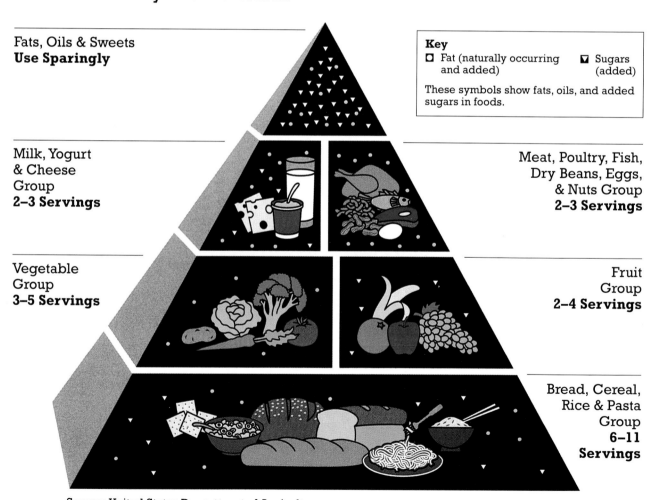

Fats, Oils & Sweets
Use Sparingly

Key
☐ Fat (naturally occurring and added) ☑ Sugars (added)

These symbols show fats, oils, and added sugars in foods.

Milk, Yogurt & Cheese Group
2–3 Servings

Meat, Poultry, Fish, Dry Beans, Eggs, & Nuts Group
2–3 Servings

Vegetable Group
3–5 Servings

Fruit Group
2–4 Servings

Bread, Cereal, Rice & Pasta Group
6–11 Servings

Source: United States Department of Agriculture

16

2 Breakfast makes a difference to your day! It fuels up your body after a good night's sleep and gives you the energy you need to do your best in school and at play. Make your morning meal fun by eating something out of the ordinary; try a favorite sandwich or yesterday's dinner, served hot or cold.

3 Snacks provide nutrients for your growing body and an energy boost between meals. Choose two or three snacks a day from the major food groups; try to keep fat, sugar, and salt to a minimum in your snacks and meals.

4 Being active helps you develop a healthy appetite. Get plenty of exercise—walk your dog, bike, roller-skate, or join a sports team. And don't forget to drink plenty of fluids to keep your body at its best.

5 Help pick out and prepare the food for family meals. You can help your brothers, sisters, and parents be their best, too.

6 At mealtime, eat slowly and stop when you feel full.

BRIGHT-EYED BREAKFASTS

Sausage Circles

These patties are perfect with our Cheddar Grits (facing page). If you don't want to use pork, just make the sausage with 1½ pounds turkey.

INGREDIENTS

8 ounces ground turkey
1 pound lean ground pork
1 teaspoon dry sage
½ teaspoon dry rosemary
¼ teaspoon pepper

EQUIPMENT

Measuring spoons
Medium-size bowl
Large frying pan
Butter knife
Utility knife
Pancake turner
Ruler
Cutting board
Serving plate

1 Place ground turkey, ground pork, sage, rosemary, and pepper in bowl and mix with your hands until well blended.

2 Use your hands to divide turkey mixture into 6 equal portions; shape each portion into a 3-inch-round patty.

3 Place frying pan on burner, add patties, and cook patties over high heat for 3 minutes. Turn patties over with pancake turner and cook for 3 more minutes.

4 Turn patties over again with pancake turner, reduce heat to medium, and cook patties for 3 more minutes. Use turner to remove one patty to cutting board; use utility knife to cut patty to center. If patty is still pink inside, return it to pan with turner; cook for about 2 more minutes, then repeat test. When patty is no longer pink inside, turn off burner and use pancake turner to place patties on serving plate.

Makes 6 patties.

Cheddar Grits

INGREDIENTS

Margarine or butter to grease baking dish

4 cups water

1 cup quick-cooking grits

2 cups (8 oz.) shredded Cheddar cheese

¼ cup margarine or butter

2 eggs

¼ cup nonfat or lowfat milk

EQUIPMENT

Measuring cups

Medium-size bowl

2- to 3-quart pan

2-quart baking dish

Butter knife

Wooden spoon

Wire rack

Oven mitts

See photograph on facing page. Grits are made from ground hominy. Mixed with cheese, they make a filling breakfast or brunch dish.

1 Preheat oven to 350°. Grease baking dish.

2 Place pan on burner, add water, and bring to a boil over medium-high heat. Slowly add grits, stirring constantly with wooden spoon; then continue to stir for about 3 minutes, until thickened. Turn off burner, add cheese and ¼ cup margarine, and mix with spoon until well blended.

3 Place eggs and milk in bowl and mix with spoon until well blended. Add a spoonful of grits to egg mixture and mix with spoon until well blended.

4 Add egg mixture to grits in pan and mix with spoon until well blended. Pour grits mixture into baking dish. Bake for about 45 minutes, until grits are golden brown on top. Turn off oven and use mitts to remove baking dish to rack.

Makes 6 servings.

TELL A FRIEND THAT...
Cheddar cheese was first made in Cheddar, England, with cheese-making techniques the colonists brought to North America in the 1700s. Cheese is a source of calcium, especially important for building strong bones and teeth as you grow.

SUPER HERO

STRONG ENOUGH!

PRETTY GOOD!

TRY AGAIN!

HIT HERE

Garden Variety Omelet

You may add other garden favorites, such as green bell pepper or zucchini, to this omelet's fresh tomato and cheese filling.

INGREDIENTS

1 pear-shaped tomato

3 eggs

1 tablespoon water

½ teaspoon dry oregano

¼ teaspoon pepper

1 tablespoon margarine or butter

¼ cup shredded jack cheese

EQUIPMENT

Measuring cups

Measuring spoons

Medium-size bowl

Small nonstick frying pan

Butter knife

Utility knife

Fork

Pancake turner

Cutting board

Serving plate

1 Use utility knife to cut tomato in half lengthwise on cutting board. Place each half cut side down and cut lengthwise into thin strips. Then cut strips crosswise into small chunks.

2 Separate 2 of the eggs and reserve yolks for another use; place egg whites in bowl. Add remaining whole egg, water, oregano, and pepper to bowl and mix with fork until well blended.

3 Place frying pan on burner, add margarine, and melt over medium-high heat. Add egg mixture to pan all at once.

4 When edges of egg mixture begin to set (this will happen almost at once), lift egg with pancake turner. Tilt pan toward edge you have lifted to let uncooked egg flow underneath cooked portion; then place pan back completely on burner.

5 When omelet is completely set (no egg flows if you shake pan), turn off burner. Tilt pan over serving plate and let omelet slide onto plate. Sprinkle tomato and cheese on one half of omelet; fold other half of omelet over filling.

Makes 1 serving.

All-in-One Oatmeal

No need to pour a glass of juice with this breakfast! Each bowlful of hot cereal comes with its own burst of orange.

INGREDIENTS

1½ cups regular rolled oats

1 tablespoon firmly packed brown sugar

⅛ teaspoon ground cloves

3 cups orange juice

2 tablespoons currants or dried mixed fruit bits

EQUIPMENT

Measuring cups

Measuring spoons

2- to 3-quart pan & lid

Butter knife

Wooden spoon

1 Place oats, brown sugar, and cloves in pan and mix with wooden spoon until blended. Add orange juice and currants and mix with spoon until well blended.

2 Place pan on burner and bring oat mixture to a boil over medium-high heat, stirring occasionally. Reduce heat to low and continue to stir occasionally for 5 minutes. Turn off burner, cover pan, and let stand for 5 minutes.

Makes 4 servings.

Berryful Muffins

INGREDIENTS

1 cup all-purpose flour

½ cup whole wheat flour

2 teaspoons baking powder

1 teaspoon baking soda

½ teaspoon salt

½ teaspoon ground nutmeg

1 egg

¼ cup salad oil

½ cup sugar

¾ cup nonfat or lowfat milk

2 cups fresh or frozen
   blueberries

EQUIPMENT

Measuring cups

Measuring spoons

Medium-size bowl

Large bowl

Muffin pan

Butter knife

Utility spoon

Rubber spatula

Wire rack

Oven mitts

12 paper muffin cups

Barely mix the batter to keep these muffins tender and even-textured. Add plenty of fresh or frozen blueberries!

1 Preheat oven to 375°. Line muffin pan with paper muffin cups.

2 Place all-purpose flour, whole wheat flour, baking powder, baking soda, salt, and nutmeg in large bowl and mix with utility spoon until well blended.

3 Place egg, oil, sugar, and milk in medium-size bowl and mix with spoon until well blended.

4 Pour egg mixture all at once into flour mixture and mix with spoon just until flour is evenly moistened. Add blueberries and use spatula to fold berries gently into batter. Batter will be lumpy.

5 Spoon batter into muffin cups until each cup is three-fourths full. Bake for about 20 minutes, until muffins are lightly browned.

6 Turn off oven and use mitts to remove muffin pan. Immediately turn pan upside down above rack so muffins slide out. Turn muffins right side up and serve.

Makes 12 muffins.

Lemon-Strawberry Waffles

No one will guess the secret ingredient in your waffles—it's lemon yogurt! For variety, try another flavor of yogurt or use a different berry on top.

INGREDIENTS

3 cups strawberries

½ cup margarine or butter, at room temperature

2 cups all-purpose flour

1 teaspoon baking powder

1 teaspoon baking soda

¼ teaspoon salt

2 cups nonfat or lowfat lemon yogurt

2 eggs

EQUIPMENT

Measuring cups

Measuring spoons

Medium-size bowl

Large bowl

Small frying pan

Waffle iron

Butter knife

Utility knife

Fork

Utility spoon

Whisk

Cutting board

Serving bowl

Serving plates

TELL A FRIEND THAT...
the Native Americans grew strawberries and shared them with new settlers in Massachusetts during the mid-1600s. High in vitamin C, strawberries can help keep your gums healthy.

1 Turn on waffle iron, following manufacturer's instructions.

2 Use utility knife to cut tops off strawberries on cutting board. Cut berries into thin slices and place in serving bowl.

3 Place frying pan on burner, add margarine, and melt slowly over low heat. Turn off burner.

4 Place flour, baking powder, baking soda, and salt in large bowl and mix with whisk until well blended.

5 Place yogurt and eggs in medium-size bowl and mix with whisk until blended; add to flour mixture and mix with whisk until well blended.

6 Add melted margarine to batter and mix with whisk until well blended.

7 Use utility spoon to place about ¾ cup batter on center of waffle iron; close iron and cook for about 5 minutes, until steaming stops. Carefully open iron and use fork to remove waffle to serving plate.

8 Repeat step 7 until all batter is used. Turn off waffle iron. Serve waffles with strawberries.

Makes 12 waffles.

Ginger Peachy Coffeecake

Get your hands into the action when you make the sweet crumb topping for this quick cake.

INGREDIENTS

Margarine or butter to grease baking pan

3 peaches (about 1 lb. *total*)

3¼ cups all-purpose flour

1¾ cups firmly packed brown sugar

¾ cup regular rolled oats

2 teaspoons ground cinnamon

½ cup margarine or butter, at room temperature

1 tablespoon baking powder

½ teaspoon baking soda

½ teaspoon salt

1 teaspoon ground ginger

1 cup buttermilk

2 eggs

½ cup salad oil

EQUIPMENT

Measuring cups

Measuring spoons

2 medium-size bowls

Large bowl

9- by 13-inch baking pan

Butter knife

Utility knife

Utility spoon

Rubber spatula

Wooden pick

Cutting board

Wire rack

Oven mitts

TELL A FRIEND THAT. . . peaches were probably first grown several thousand years ago in China. Like other fruits and vegetables, peaches carry their vitamins close to their skins—so to get the most out of them, eat them unpeeled.

1 Preheat oven to 375°. Grease baking pan.

2 Use utility knife to cut peaches into thin slices on cutting board. Pull slices off pits with your fingers; set aside on board.

3 To make crumb topping, place ¾ cup of the flour, ¾ cup of the brown sugar, oats, cinnamon, and ½ cup margarine in one medium-size bowl. Mix with your fingers until well blended.

4 Place remaining 2½ cups flour, remaining 1 cup brown sugar, baking powder, baking soda, salt, and ginger in large bowl and mix with utility spoon until well blended.

5 Place buttermilk, eggs, and oil in second medium-size bowl and mix with spoon until well blended.

6 Add buttermilk mixture to flour mixture in large bowl and mix with spoon just until flour is evenly moistened. Add peaches and use spatula to fold fruit gently into batter.

7 Pour batter into baking pan, scraping out bowl with spatula; sprinkle with crumb topping. Bake for about 35 minutes, until wooden pick inserted in center of cake comes out clean. Turn off oven and use mitts to remove pan to rack.

Makes 12 to 16 servings.

29

Allspice Baked Apples

If you have eaten all your homemade Dawn-to-Dusk Granola (page 72), fill these honey-sweetened apples with a store-bought variety.

1 Preheat oven to 350°.

2 Place granola and allspice in bowl and mix with utility spoon until well blended.

3 Push corer through center of each apple; twist corer and pull out apple core. Discard core. Place cored apples in baking pan and use spoon to fill hole in center of each apple with granola mixture. Mound remaining granola mixture evenly on top of apples.

4 Place orange juice and honey in bowl and mix with spoon until well blended. Pour juice mixture over each apple (mixture will overflow into pan).

5 Cover pan with foil; fold foil around pan edges to seal. Bake for 1 hour. Turn off oven and use mitts to remove pan to rack. Carefully remove foil, starting on a side away from you to avoid steam. Use tongs to remove apples gently from pan and place them on serving plates. Spoon juice mixture from pan over each apple.

Makes 6 servings.

INGREDIENTS

1 cup granola

⅛ teaspoon ground allspice

6 medium-size Granny
    Smith apples

¾ cup orange juice

¼ cup honey

EQUIPMENT

Measuring cups

Measuring spoons

Small bowl

9-inch-square baking pan

Butter knife

Utility spoon

Apple corer

Tongs

Wire rack

Oven mitts

Foil

Serving plates

Too Two Smoothie

Easy to make and to remember, this breakfast drink takes two of each ingredient.

INGREDIENTS
2 bananas
2 cups orange juice
2 ice cubes

EQUIPMENT
Measuring cups
Blender

1 Peel bananas, break into chunks, and place in blender. Add orange juice and ice cubes; cover and whirl until well blended.

Makes 4 servings.

Mixed Berry Yogurt Topping

Granola is the secret to this topping. Spread it on rice cakes for a quick, tasty start to the day.

INGREDIENTS
1 cup nonfat or lowfat
   mixed berry yogurt
1 cup granola

EQUIPMENT
Measuring cups
Medium-size bowl
Butter knife
Utility spoon

1 Place yogurt and granola in bowl and mix with utility spoon until well blended.

Makes 1½ cups (about 12 servings).

MENU

Ginger Peachy Coffeecake (page 28)

Ham & Eggs Pie (page 43)

Fancy Fruit Salad (page 42)

Too Two Smoothie (page 31)

Breakfast in Bed

Pamper one person or pile the whole family into bed for this breakfast.

Do most of the work the day before:

- Prepare Ginger Peachy Coffeecake and Ham & Eggs Pie.

- Make trays by tucking shirt box bottoms into tops; color insides of trays.

- Make vases by pasting colored paper on empty juice cans.

- Make flowers by twisting pipe cleaner stems around colored tissue-paper petals. Place flowers in vases.

- Write cards or poems for reading material.

Finish the work that morning:

- Put napkins, utensils, vases, and reading material on trays.

- Prepare Fancy Fruit Salad and Too Two Smoothie; pour juice into glasses.

- Place heaping helpings of fruit salad and a slice each of coffeecake and pie on plates. Place plates and glasses on trays and carefully carry trays to bed.

LIP-SMACKING LUNCHES

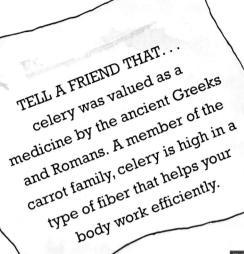

Tuna-stuffed Pockets

See photograph on facing page. You can carry your lunch anywhere when you tuck tuna filling into an edible envelope of pita bread.

INGREDIENTS

1 large can (12½ oz.) solid white tuna packed in water

6 tablespoons mayonnaise

1 lemon

½ teaspoon curry powder

2 celery stalks

¼ cup unsalted sunflower seeds

4 butter lettuce leaves

4 whole wheat pita breads

EQUIPMENT

Measuring cups

Measuring spoons

Medium-size bowl

Butter knife

Utility knife

Utility spoon

Juicer

Can opener

Cutting board

Paper towels

1 Use can opener to open can of tuna about three-fourths of the way around; drain off liquid by pressing down firmly on center of lid and holding can upside down over sink. Use opener to open can completely; put tuna in bowl. Add mayonnaise to bowl and mix with utility spoon until well blended.

2 Use utility knife to cut lemon in half crosswise on cutting board. Use juicer to squeeze 2 tablespoons juice from lemon. Add lemon juice and curry powder to tuna mixture in bowl and mix with spoon until well blended.

3 Use utility knife to cut celery crosswise on cutting board into thin slices. Add celery and sunflower seeds to tuna mixture and mix with spoon until well blended.

4 Rinse each lettuce leaf in cold water and shake off as much water as you can; then drain lettuce on paper towels. Use utility knife to cut a thin slice off top of each pita bread on cutting board. Tuck a lettuce leaf into each pita bread, then spoon in a fourth of the tuna mixture.

Makes 4 sandwiches.

Say Cheese & Smile Sandwiches

Creamy cheese and peanut butter faces will make you smile too, because they're so easy to create.

INGREDIENTS

½ cup old-fashioned chunky peanut butter

3 ounces Neufchâtel cheese, at room temperature

2 tablespoons honey

4 slices raisin bread

1 banana

¼ cup raisins

EQUIPMENT

Measuring cups

Measuring spoons

Medium-size bowl

Butter knife

Utility spoon

Cutting board

1 Place peanut butter, Neufchâtel cheese, and honey in bowl and mix with utility spoon until well blended.

2 Use butter knife to spread peanut butter mixture on each slice of bread. Peel banana and use knife to cut banana crosswise on cutting board into 12 equal pieces. Place banana pieces on peanut butter mixture to look like eyes and a nose. Arrange raisins on peanut butter mixture to make a smile.

Makes 4 sandwiches.

Can't Top It Pizza

Here's a pizza with tomatoes, but without the sauce. You can add even more toppings—how about sliced mushrooms?

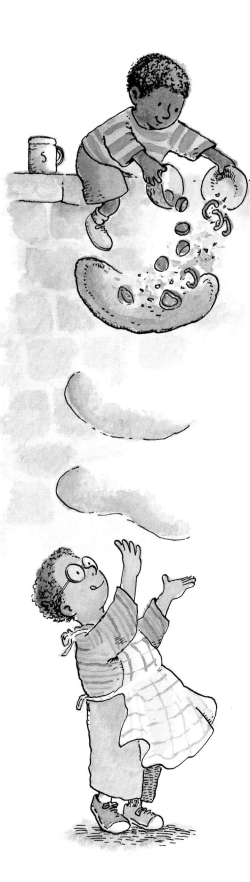

INGREDIENTS

2 cups all-purpose flour

1 teaspoon salt

1 teaspoon sugar

1 package active dry yeast

¾ cup water, warm to touch

All-purpose flour to flour work surface

Salad oil to grease bowl and pizza pan

1 cup cherry tomatoes

1 green or yellow bell pepper

1 cup (4 oz.) shredded part-skim mozzarella cheese

½ cup grated Parmesan cheese

1 teaspoon dry basil

EQUIPMENT

Measuring cups

Measuring spoons

Medium-size bowl

Large bowl

14-inch pizza pan

Butter knife

Utility knife

Utility spoon

Pancake turner

Rolling pin

Cutting board

Wire rack

Oven mitts

Towel

1 Place 2 cups flour in medium-size bowl and make a well with your hands; add salt, sugar, and yeast to well. Add warm water to well and let stand for about 10 minutes, until yeast is bubbly. Mix yeast mixture into flour with utility spoon until well blended.

2 Lightly flour a work surface. Place dough on work surface. Push dough away from you with the heel of your hand; grab the farthest edge of dough with your fingers and pull dough over itself and back to you. Turn dough slightly clockwise and repeat these kneading steps for 15 minutes, adding flour as needed to keep dough from sticking to surface. Shape dough into a ball, then stick your finger into it; if the hole closes up almost at once, dough is ready to rise. If hole doesn't close up quickly, knead dough for a few more minutes. Shape dough into a ball; lightly grease large bowl with oil, place dough in bowl, and turn dough over to coat with oil. Cover bowl with towel and let dough rise in a warm place for about 2 hours, until doubled in size.

3 Meanwhile, use utility knife to cut cherry tomatoes in half lengthwise on cutting board. Use utility knife to cut top off bell pepper on cutting board; remove seeds with your fingers and cut pepper crosswise into thin slices.

4 Preheat oven to 425°. Grease pizza pan with oil. After dough has risen, punch it down with your fist and return it to lightly floured work surface. Set rolling pin on center of dough and roll out from center to edges to make a circle slightly larger than pan. Fold dough in half, pick it up, and place in pan (dough will hang over edge of pan). Unfold dough; then roll overhang over itself to form an edge in pan.

5 Cover dough with mozzarella cheese, cherry tomato halves (cut side up), bell pepper slices, Parmesan cheese, and basil. With your fingers, lightly coat dough edge with oil. Bake for about 20 minutes, until edge is lightly browned. Turn off oven and use mitts to remove pan to rack. Use pancake turner to remove pizza to cleaned cutting board. Use utility knife to cut pizza into wedges.

Makes 8 servings.

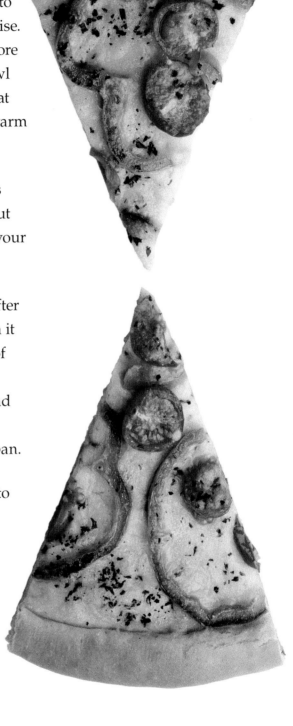

You're the Chef Salad

Pick and choose your favorite salad ingredients to make this fresh green salad tossed with meat and cheese.

INGREDIENTS

1 small head romaine lettuce; or 1 large head loose-leaf lettuce, such as red leaf or butter lettuce

8 ounces spinach

1 yellow or red bell pepper

2 cups red or yellow cherry tomatoes

1 can (about 15½ oz.) reduced-sodium garbanzo beans

4 ounces cooked turkey or chicken breast

4 ounces smoked turkey or chicken breast

4 ounces Swiss cheese

3 lemons

½ cup salad oil

Salt and pepper, if you like

EQUIPMENT

Measuring cups

Small bowl

Large bowl

Utility knife

Whisk

Juicer

Can opener

Ruler

Colander

Cutting board

Paper towels

Plastic bag

Serving spoons

1 Half-fill sink with cool water. Break lettuce leaves from core and drop into water. Remove tough stems and midribs from spinach leaves; add spinach leaves to water with lettuce. Shake lettuce and spinach leaves in water to rinse well; then place leaves on paper towels, wrap gently, put in plastic bag, and refrigerate for 30 minutes.

2 Use utility knife to cut top off bell pepper on cutting board; cut pepper in half lengthwise and remove seeds with your fingers. Cut each pepper half crosswise into ¼-inch-thick slices; place in large bowl. Add cherry tomatoes to bowl.

3 Place beans in colander and rinse with water until water runs clear. Add beans to bowl.

4 Place turkey, smoked turkey, and cheese on cutting board. Use utility knife to cut meats and cheese into strips about ¼ inch thick, ½ inch wide, and 2 inches long. Add meats and cheese to bowl.

5 Tear lettuce and spinach leaves into bite-size pieces and add to bowl.

6 Use utility knife to cut lemons in half crosswise on cutting board; use juicer to squeeze ½ cup juice from lemons. Place lemon juice and oil in small bowl and mix with whisk until well blended. Pour dressing over salad; toss salad with serving spoons. Add salt and pepper, if you like.

Makes 4 servings.

Fancy Fruit Salad

For a pretty look, surround each serving of salad with mandarin orange segments, arranged in a pinwheel pattern.

INGREDIENTS

1 cup strawberries

1 cup nonfat or lowfat plain yogurt

1 tablespoon honey

1 cup raspberries

1 cup blackberries

1 cup blueberries

1 cup seedless red grapes

⅓ cup walnut pieces

EQUIPMENT

Measuring cups

Measuring spoons

Large bowl

Utility spoon

Potato masher

1 Pull leaves off strawberries and place strawberries in bowl. Use potato masher to mash strawberries into pulp. Add yogurt and honey and mix with utility spoon until well blended.

2 Add raspberries, blackberries, blueberries, and grapes to bowl and gently mix with spoon. Top with walnut pieces.

Makes 4 servings.

Ham & Eggs Pie

INGREDIENTS

Margarine or butter to grease pie pan

1 slice whole wheat bread

4 ounces Canadian bacon

1 cup (4 oz.) shredded part-skim mozzarella cheese

1 sprig parsley

2 cups (about 1 lb.) nonfat or lowfat cottage cheese

3 eggs

EQUIPMENT

Measuring cups

9-inch pie pan

Blender or food processor

Butter knife

Utility knife

Rubber spatula

Ruler

Cutting board

Wire rack

Oven mitts

See photograph on facing page. Quick quiche tastes yummy hot or (if any is leftover) cold from the refrigerator.

 Preheat oven to 350°. Grease pie pan.

2 Tear bread into pieces, place in blender, cover, and whirl until blended into crumbs. Pour crumbs into pan and tilt pan from side to side to cover bottom and sides completely with crumbs.

3 Use utility knife to cut bacon into ¼-inch strips on cutting board; cut strips crosswise into ¼-inch squares. Sprinkle bacon and mozzarella cheese into pan.

4 Place parsley, cottage cheese, and eggs in blender, cover, and whirl until well blended. Pour into pan, scraping out blender with spatula. Smooth top of pie with spatula. Bake for about 35 minutes, until pie is golden and butter knife blade inserted in center comes out clean. Turn off oven and use mitts to remove pan to rack. Let pie stand for 5 minutes before serving.

Makes 6 to 8 servings.

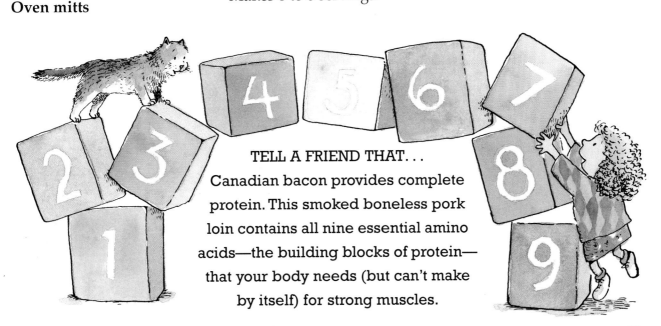

TELL A FRIEND THAT...
Canadian bacon provides complete protein. This smoked boneless pork loin contains all nine essential amino acids—the building blocks of protein—that your body needs (but can't make by itself) for strong muscles.

INGREDIENTS

2 slices whole wheat bread

¼ cup cornmeal

¼ cup grated Parmesan cheese

½ teaspoon dry marjoram

½ teaspoon dry thyme

¼ teaspoon dry sage

¼ teaspoon pepper

1 egg

1 tablespoon water

4 skinless, boneless chicken breast halves

EQUIPMENT

Measuring cups

Measuring spoons

Small bowl

Medium-size bowl

10- by 15-inch baking pan

Blender or food processor

Butter knife

Utility knife

Fork

Pancake turner

Cutting board

Wire rack

Oven mitts

Foil

Paper towels

Lazy Day Chicken

See photograph on facing page. When it's too hot to cook, you'll be glad you planned ahead and can reach into the refrigerator for this crunchy baked chicken.

1 Preheat oven to 450°.

2 Tear bread into pieces, place in blender, cover, and whirl until blended into crumbs. Place crumbs, cornmeal, cheese, marjoram, thyme, sage, and pepper in medium-size bowl and mix with fork until well blended.

3 Place egg and water in small bowl and mix with fork until well blended.

4 Rinse chicken in cold water and pat dry with paper towels. Dip both sides of each chicken piece first in egg mixture, then in crumb mixture; place in baking pan. Top chicken with any remaining crumb mixture and bake for 20 minutes. Use mitts to remove pan from oven to rack. Use pancake turner to lift one piece of chicken to cutting board; use utility knife to cut chicken to center of thickest part. If chicken is still pink inside, return it to pan with turner. Use mitts to return pan to oven. Bake for about 5 more minutes; then repeat test. When chicken is no longer pink inside, turn off oven. Let chicken cool slightly, wrap in foil, and refrigerate for at least 6 hours or until next day.

Makes 4 servings.

Already Ready Soup

Vegetable soup ready in minutes! The secret is starting with stewed tomatoes.

INGREDIENTS

1 can (about 14½ oz.) no-salt-added stewed tomatoes

3 cans (14½ oz. *each*) reduced-sodium chicken broth

½ cup quick-cooking pearl barley

1 package (10 oz.) frozen corn kernels

1 package (9 oz.) frozen cut green beans

8 ounces frozen baby carrots

1 teaspoon dry oregano

¼ teaspoon pepper

EQUIPMENT

Measuring cups

Measuring spoons

4- to 5-quart pan & lid

Butter knife

Wooden spoon

Can opener

1 Place pan on burner, add stewed tomatoes and chicken broth, and bring to a boil over high heat, stirring occasionally with wooden spoon.

2 Add barley, corn, beans, carrots, oregano, and pepper to pan. Reduce heat to medium-low, cover, and simmer for 10 minutes, stirring occasionally. Turn off burner and serve.

Makes 6 to 8 servings.

INGREDIENTS

1 cup catsup

½ cup firmly packed brown
   sugar

1 tablespoon dry mustard

1½ teaspoons
   Worcestershire sauce

12 green onions

1 cup regular rolled oats

¼ teaspoon pepper

1 egg

1½ pounds lean ground
   beef

16 slices multigrain bread

EQUIPMENT

Measuring cups

Measuring spoons

Medium-size bowl

Large bowl

5- by 9-inch loaf pan

Butter knife

Utility knife

Fork

Cutting board

Wire rack

Oven mitts

Foil

Made-ahead Meat Loaf

See photograph on facing page. Delicious hot, this meat loaf improves with age. Try waiting until tomorrow to eat cold slices in sandwiches.

1 Preheat oven to 350°. Place catsup, brown sugar, mustard, and Worcestershire sauce in medium-size bowl and mix with fork until well blended.

2 Place green onions on cutting board. Use utility knife to cut onions (including some green part) crosswise into enough thin slices to make ½ cup. Place onions, oats, pepper, and egg in large bowl and mix with fork until blended. Add ½ cup of the catsup mixture and mix until blended. Add ground beef and mix with your hands until well blended.

3 Use your hands to pat meat mixture evenly into loaf pan. Bake for 1 hour. Use mitts to remove pan to rack. Pour remaining catsup mixture over meat loaf and use mitts to return pan to oven. Bake for 15 more minutes.

4 Turn off oven and use mitts to remove pan to rack. Let cool slightly. Cover pan with foil and refrigerate until next day. Run butter knife around edges of meat loaf; then turn loaf out onto cutting board. Use butter knife to remove any fat from edges. Use utility knife to cut meat loaf crosswise into 8 thick or 16 thin slices on cutting board. Serve one thick or 2 thin slices of meat loaf between 2 slices of bread.

Makes 8 sandwiches.

TELL A FRIEND THAT. . .
rolled oats are hulled whole oats that have been steamed and flattened. Oats, a type of grain, provide carbohydrates, your body's main source of energy.

Plenty of Potatoes

Potatoes baked two times can be twice as nice to eat, especially when they come in their own edible wrappers.

INGREDIENTS

4 medium-large red thin-skinned potatoes (about 8 oz. *each*)

2 tablespoons margarine or butter

2 tablespoons nonfat or lowfat milk

1 tablespoon dried chives

¼ cup shredded Cheddar cheese

EQUIPMENT

Measuring cups

Measuring spoons

Large bowl

Rimmed baking sheet

Butter knife

Utility knife

Fork

Utility spoon

Potato masher

Cutting board

Wire rack

Oven mitts

1 Preheat oven to 400°. Rinse potatoes well with warm water; then stick each potato with fork in several places.

2 Place potatoes on baking sheet and bake for 1 hour. Use mitts to remove sheet from oven to rack. Let potatoes cool for about 10 minutes; then use mitts to lift potatoes to cutting board. Use utility knife to cut a thick slice lengthwise off top of each potato. Use utility spoon to scoop out inside of each potato slice into bowl (discard skin from potato slices). Then use spoon to scoop out center of each potato into bowl, leaving a thin shell of potato and skin.

3 Add margarine, milk, chives, and cheese to bowl and mash with potato masher until well blended. Use spoon to return potato mixture to potato shells.

4 Use mitts to place potatoes on baking sheet; return sheet to oven. Bake potatoes for about 15 minutes, until tops are golden. Turn off oven and use mitts to remove sheet to rack. Serve potatoes at once.

Makes 4 servings.

MENU

Already Ready Soup (page 45)

Tuna-stuffed Pockets (page 36)

Pass the Peanut Butter Cookies (page 84)

Really Raspberry Shake (page 75)

Rainy Day Picnic

Have a picnic even if the weather's cold and wet; just come indoors.

- Prepare Pass the Peanut Butter Cookies.

- Borrow two chairs, two blankets, and a flashlight.

- Find a warm, dry spot in your house where you are allowed to eat.

- Set the chairs back to back, allowing enough space between the chairs for you and your friends to sit down. Put one blanket down in that space. Cover the chairs with the other blanket.

- Prepare Tuna-stuffed Pockets, Really Raspberry Shake, and Already Ready Soup.

- Pour shake and soup into insulated beverage containers. Wrap sandwiches and cookies in foil or plastic wrap. Pack the food, napkins, and cups for shake and soup in a box or basket.

- Say goodbye to everyone not joining you and go off on your picnic.

- While eating, share ghost stories and make shadow figures on the blanket with your flashlight.

DOWNRIGHT DELICIOUS DINNERS

Stuffing-topped Pork Chops

INGREDIENTS

4 or 5 slices whole wheat bread

2 stalks celery

½ teaspoon dry marjoram

½ teaspoon dry sage

¼ teaspoon pepper

1 large onion

1 can (14½ oz.) reduced-sodium chicken broth

4 center-cut loin pork chops (about 1½ lbs. *total*), trimmed of fat

EQUIPMENT

Measuring cups

Measuring spoons

Large bowl

Large nonstick frying pan & lid

Butter knife

Utility knife

Wooden spoon

Pancake turner

Can opener

Ruler

Cutting board

See photograph on facing page. The delicious dressing is too good to hide inside the pork chops—just pile it on top!

1 Tear bread into about ½-inch cubes with your hands (you should have about 4 cups). Place bread in bowl. Use utility knife to cut celery crosswise into thin slices on cutting board (you should have about ½ cup); place celery in bowl. Add marjoram, sage, and pepper to bowl.

2 Use utility knife to chop onion into small pieces on cutting board. Place onion in frying pan. Place pan on burner and add ½ cup of the chicken broth. Cook over high heat, stirring often with wooden spoon, for about 5 minutes, until all liquid has cooked away. Turn off burner. Add onion and ½ cup more chicken broth to bowl; stir with spoon until stuffing is well blended.

3 Return pan to burner, add pork chops, and cook over medium-high heat for about 3 minutes. Use pancake turner to turn chops over; cook on other side for 2 minutes. Turn off burner and use spoon to pile stuffing evenly over pork chops. Pour remaining chicken broth around chops and bring to a boil over medium-high heat. Reduce heat to low, cover pan, and simmer for about 20 minutes. Turn off burner and use pancake turner to lift one pork chop to cutting board. Use utility knife to cut chop to center. If chop is still pink inside, use pancake turner to return chop to pan; cover and simmer over low heat for 5 more minutes, then repeat test. When meat is no longer pink inside, turn off burner.

Makes 4 servings.

Apple Sweet Potatoes

INGREDIENTS

1 pound sweet potatoes

1 cup apple juice

½ teaspoon ground cinnamon

EQUIPMENT

Measuring cups

Measuring spoons

2- to 3-quart pan & lid

Food processor or blender

Butter knife

Utility knife

Fork

Slotted spoon

Vegetable peeler

Ruler

Cutting board

Use either sweet potatoes or yams in this cinnamon-flavored side dish.

1 Use vegetable peeler to peel sweet potatoes. Use utility knife to cut potatoes crosswise into ½-inch-thick slices on cutting board.

2 Place pan on burner; add potatoes, apple juice, and cinnamon. Bring to a boil over high heat. Reduce heat to medium, cover pan, and cook for about 20 minutes, until potato slices are very easy to pierce with fork. Turn off burner. Use slotted spoon to lift potatoes from pan and place in food processor. Add cooking liquid from pan, cover, and whirl until well blended.

Makes 4 servings.

INGREDIENTS

2 large onions

2 pounds lean boneless beef top round

4 medium-size carrots (about 12 oz. *total*)

12 small red thin-skinned potatoes, *each* 1 to 1½ inches in diameter (about 1 lb. *total*)

1 large can (about 28 oz.) pear-shaped tomatoes

1 can (14½ oz.) beef broth

1 teaspoon dry thyme

1 bay leaf

EQUIPMENT

Measuring spoons
10- by 15-inch baking pan
12- by 17-inch baking sheet
Butter knife
Utility knife
Fork
Slotted spoon
Vegetable peeler
Can opener
Ruler
Cutting board
Wire rack
Oven mitts
Foil

Windy Weather Stew

See photograph on facing page. Put aside some time on a cold, windy day to make a slowly baked beef stew that will warm up any family get-together.

1 Preheat oven to 450°.

2 Use utility knife to chop onions into small pieces on cutting board. Place onions in baking pan.

3 Use utility knife to cut beef into 1-inch strips on cutting board; cut strips into 1-inch chunks. Peel carrots and use utility knife to cut carrots crosswise into ½-inch slices on cutting board. Rinse potatoes well with warm water.

4 Pour tomatoes and their liquid into pan; break tomatoes into smaller pieces with slotted spoon. Add beef, carrots, potatoes, beef broth, thyme, and bay leaf and mix with spoon until blended. Cover pan with foil and fold foil around pan edges to seal. Place pan in oven; place baking sheet on rack below pan to catch any drips. Bake stew for 2¾ hours. Use mitts to remove pan to rack; carefully remove foil, starting on a side away from you to avoid steam. Use slotted spoon to remove a beef chunk and a potato to cutting board. Use utility knife to cut beef to center; use fork to pierce potato. If meat is still pink inside and potato is difficult to pierce, return both to pan. Cover again and use mitts to return pan to oven; bake for 5 more minutes, then repeat test. When meat and potatoes are done, turn off oven.

Makes 6 servings.

INGREDIENTS

1½ pounds broccoli, baby carrots, or green beans

EQUIPMENT

Measuring cup

Large frying pan & lid

Rack to fit in frying pan

Utility knife

Fork

Tongs

Ruler

Cutting board

Serving plate

TELL A FRIEND THAT. . . broccoli was a favorite of the ancient Romans. Like other dark-colored vegetables and fruits, broccoli is packed with vitamins and minerals to help you maintain good health.

Simply Steamed Veggies

You can top your vegetables with melted margarine or butter mixed with a little lemon juice and pepper, but they are also delicious served completely plain.

1 Place broccoli on cutting board. Use utility knife to cut off base of broccoli stalks, leaving about 3 inches of stalks below flowerets; discard base. Use utility knife to cut stalk and flowerets lengthwise into spears. Cut base of each spear lengthwise about 1 inch up toward flowerets. (If using carrots, leave whole. If using beans, use utility knife to cut off ends on cutting board; then cut beans into 2-inch lengths.)

2 Place rack in frying pan. Use measuring cup to add 1 to 1½ inches water to pan, making sure water does not come up to bottom of rack. Place pan on burner and bring water to a boil over high heat. Use tongs to place vegetables carefully and evenly on rack; cover and cook for 8 minutes. Turn off burner. Carefully remove lid from pan, tilting it away from you to avoid steam. Stick fork into a broccoli spear, carrot, or bean. If vegetable is not tender, cover pan, return to high heat, and cook for about 2 more minutes. Turn off burner, carefully remove lid from pan (watch out for steam), and repeat test. When vegetables are tender, remove with tongs to serving plate.

Makes 6 servings.

Colorful Swordfish Kebabs

See photograph on facing page. Serve these tasty skewers of fish, tomatoes, and bell peppers with Ready Rice Pilaf (facing page).

INGREDIENTS

1 pound swordfish, cut
    1 inch thick

1 medium-size onion

1 clove garlic

1 lemon

1 tablespoon salad oil

¼ cup reduced-sodium
    chicken broth

1 teaspoon dry oregano

1 green bell pepper

8 cherry tomatoes

EQUIPMENT

Measuring cups

Measuring spoons

Broiler pan

Butter knife

Utility knife

Fork

Garlic press

Juicer

Can opener

4 metal skewers, about
    10 inches long

Cutting board

Wire rack

Oven mitts

Foil

Paper towels

Sealable 1-gallon
    plastic bag

1 Rinse swordfish with cold water and pat dry with paper towels. Use utility knife to cut swordfish into 20 equal-size pieces on cutting board.

2 Use utility knife to chop onion into small pieces on cutting board; place in plastic bag. Squeeze garlic through press into bag. Use utility knife to cut lemon in half crosswise on cutting board; use juicer to squeeze 2 tablespoons juice from lemon. Add lemon juice, oil, chicken broth, and oregano to bag. Place swordfish in bag; then seal bag and shake to blend ingredients and coat fish. Set bag of fish in broiler pan; refrigerate for 1 to 2 hours, turning bag over occasionally.

3 Remove fish from refrigerator. Position oven rack so top of broiler pan is 4 inches below heat source. Remove pan from oven; preheat oven to broil.

4 Use utility knife to cut top off bell pepper on cutting board; cut pepper in half lengthwise and remove seeds with your fingers. Cut each pepper half lengthwise in half; then cut each pepper piece in half crosswise (you will have a total of 8 pepper pieces).

5 Line broiler pan with foil. Remove fish from marinade. Carefully thread one skewer in this order: fish cube, tomato, fish cube, pepper piece, fish cube, tomato, fish cube, pepper piece, fish cube. Thread remaining 3 skewers the same way. Place skewers in broiler pan. Broil for 5 minutes. Use oven mitts to remove pan to rack and carefully turn skewers over; use oven mitts to return pan to oven. Broil for 5 more minutes and use mitts to return pan to rack.

6 Use fork to pierce fish in thickest part. If fish does not flake, use mitts to return pan to oven for about 2 more minutes; then repeat test. When fish flakes, turn off oven.

Makes 4 servings.

Ready Rice Pilaf

INGREDIENTS
1 small onion

**1 can (14½ oz.) reduced-
    sodium chicken broth**

¾ cup brown rice

EQUIPMENT
Measuring cups

1½- to 2-quart pan & lid

Butter knife

Utility knife

Wooden spoon

Can opener

Cutting board

Easy-to-prepare pilaf is the perfect choice to accompany both everyday and elegant main dishes.

1 Use utility knife to chop onion into small pieces on cutting board. Place onion in pan. Place pan on burner and add ¼ cup of the chicken broth. Cook over high heat, stirring often with wooden spoon, for about 4 minutes, until almost all liquid has cooked away. Add rice and continue to cook for 1 more minute, stirring occasionally.

2 Add remaining chicken broth and bring to a boil; reduce heat to low, cover pan, and cook for about 40 minutes, until all liquid is absorbed. Turn off burner and let stand, covered, for 10 minutes.

Makes 4 servings.

Speedy Shrimp Stir-fry

INGREDIENTS

12 ounces fresh snow peas or 2 packages (6 oz. *each*) frozen snow peas

1 can (about 8 oz.) sliced water chestnuts

1 large red bell pepper

2 green onions

2 teaspoons cornstarch

1 teaspoon sugar

¼ teaspoon ground ginger

½ cup reduced-sodium chicken broth

2 tablespoons reduced-sodium soy sauce

1 tablespoon rice vinegar

8 ounces small cooked, shelled shrimp

EQUIPMENT

Measuring cups

Measuring spoons

Small bowl

Large frying pan

Butter knife

Utility knife

Wooden spoon

Whisk

Can opener

Colander

Cutting board

Once you have all your ingredients ready to go, this meal can be on the table in minutes! For fun, try making it in a wok.

1 If you are using fresh snow peas, remove ends and strings of pods with your hands. Place snow peas in colander and rinse. Add water chestnuts to colander to drain.

2 Use utility knife to cut top off bell pepper on cutting board; cut pepper in half lengthwise and remove seeds with your fingers. Cut each pepper half crosswise into thin strips. Use utility knife to cut green onions (including some green part) crosswise into thin slices on cutting board.

3 Place cornstarch, sugar, ginger, chicken broth, soy sauce, and vinegar in bowl and mix with whisk until well blended. Place frying pan on burner, add broth mixture, and bring to a boil over high heat, stirring occasionally with wooden spoon. Add bell pepper, green onions, fresh or frozen snow peas, water chestnuts, and shrimp; stir with spoon for about 2 minutes, until mixture is well blended and heated through. Turn off burner.

Makes 4 servings.

Corny Chili

INGREDIENTS

2 cans (about 15 oz. *each*)
   black beans

1 large onion

1 clove garlic

1 pound ground turkey

3 tablespoons chili powder

1 large can (about 28 oz.)
   tomatoes

1 small can (about 4 oz.)
   diced green chiles

1 package (10 oz.) frozen
   corn kernels

EQUIPMENT

Measuring spoons

4- to 5-quart pan

Butter knife

Utility knife

Wooden spoon

Garlic press

Can opener

Colander

Cutting board

For a change, try replacing the black beans in this recipe with red or white kidney beans (or combine two different kinds of beans).

1 Place beans in colander and rinse with water until water runs clear.

2 Use utility knife to chop onion into small pieces on cutting board; place in pan. Squeeze garlic through press into pan. Place pan on burner and crumble in turkey. Cook over medium-high heat, stirring occasionally with wooden spoon, for about 5 minutes, until turkey is no longer pink.

3 Add chili powder, tomatoes (break them up with wooden spoon) and their liquid, chiles, corn, and beans to pan. Reduce heat to medium-low and simmer, uncovered, for 15 minutes.

Makes 4 servings.

Layered Spinach Lasagne

It's easy to build this lasagne—just stack up sauce, noodles, and filling. Then relax; the pasta cooks right in the baking pan!

INGREDIENTS

1 package (10 oz.) frozen chopped spinach, thawed

4 cups (about 2 lbs.) part-skim ricotta cheese

½ teaspoon ground nutmeg

1 large onion

1 clove garlic

1 can (14½ oz.) reduced-sodium chicken broth

2 large cans (15 oz. *each*) no-salt-added tomato sauce

1 can (6 oz.) tomato paste

1 teaspoon dry oregano

¼ teaspoon pepper

1 package (8 oz.) dry lasagne noodles

2 cups (8 oz.) shredded part-skim mozzarella cheese

½ cup grated Parmesan cheese

EQUIPMENT

Measuring cups

Measuring spoons

Large bowl

Large frying pan

9- by 13-inch baking pan

12- by 17-inch baking pan

Butter knife

Utility knife

Wooden spoon

Garlic press

Can opener

Cutting board

Wire rack

Oven mitts

Foil

TELL A FRIEND THAT...
spinach was grown in ancient Persia over 2,000 years ago. Cooked, it's a good source of potassium, important for muscle and nerve function.

1 Preheat oven to 375°.

2 Use your hands to squeeze as much liquid as you can out of spinach. Place spinach, ricotta cheese, and nutmeg in bowl and mix with wooden spoon until well blended.

3 Use utility knife to chop onion into small pieces on cutting board. Place onion in frying pan. Squeeze garlic through press into pan. Place pan on burner and add ½ cup of the chicken broth. Cook over high heat, stirring often with spoon, for about 5 minutes, until all liquid has cooked away. Turn off burner. Add remaining chicken broth, tomato sauce, tomato paste, oregano, and pepper to pan; stir to blend.

4 Spread 1½ cups of the sauce in 9- by 13-inch baking pan. Arrange a third of the noodles evenly over sauce, spread half the ricotta mixture over noodles, and top with a third each of the mozzarella and Parmesan cheeses. Repeat layers of sauce, noodles, ricotta mixture, mozzarella cheese, and Parmesan cheese once. Top with 1½ cups more sauce; then layer remaining noodles, sauce, mozzarella cheese, and Parmesan cheese on top. Carefully cover pan with foil and fold foil around pan edges to seal.

5 Set pan of lasagne in 12- by 17-inch baking pan to catch any drips. Bake for 45 minutes; then use mitts to remove pan to rack. Carefully remove foil, starting on a side away from you to avoid steam. Use mitts to return pan to oven and bake, uncovered, for about 15 more minutes, until top is golden. Turn off oven and use mitts to remove pan to rack. Let stand for 5 minutes before serving.

Makes 8 servings.

MENU

Colorful Swordfish Kebabs (page 56)

Ready Rice Pilaf (page 57)

Simply Steamed Carrots (page 55)

Double-dipped Strawberries (page 80)

PROPER DRESS REQUIRED FOR EVERYONE EATING HERE.

Menu

Dress-up Dinner

Create a four-star meal delicious enough to impress any critic!

- Ask everyone to dress for a special dinner.

- Write the menu in your fanciest writing on a piece of paper.

- Make place mats by coloring pieces of paper. Find a pretty tablecloth.

- About 2 hours before dinner, marinate the swordfish.

- Prepare Double-dipped Strawberries and choose a special serving plate for them.

- Set the table with the tablecloth, place mats, plates, glasses, and utensils.

- Stuff center of each napkin in a glass, letting ends hang over sides of glass.

- Place menu in center of table.

- Prepare Ready Rice Pilaf, Colorful Swordfish Kebabs, and Simply Steamed Carrots.

- Welcome everyone to dinner and explain the menu.

- Help serve the meal and be sure to offer seconds of strawberries.

- Treat everyone to a bit of entertainment during dinner by playing an instrument or singing a song.

PLEASE WAIT TO BE SEATED !

SUPER STAR SNACKS

Alphabet Bread

Write your own messages with these cheese-filled letters made from frozen bread dough. Be sure you allow enough time to thaw the dough — it takes an hour or two at room temperature, or overnight in the refrigerator.

INGREDIENTS

Margarine or butter to grease baking sheets

All-purpose flour to flour work surface

1 pound frozen whole wheat bread dough, thawed

1 cup (4 oz.) shredded Cheddar cheese

EQUIPMENT

Measuring cups

Measuring spoons

Two 12- by 15-inch baking sheets

Butter knife

Ruler

Rolling pin

Wire racks

Oven mitts

1 Grease baking sheets.

2 Lightly flour a large work surface. Place dough on surface and use rolling pin to roll dough into a 6- by 36-inch rectangle. Use butter knife to cut dough into twelve 3- by 6-inch rectangles. Place 1 heaping tablespoon cheese in middle of each rectangle. Fold one long side of each rectangle over cheese to meet other long side; pinch together to close, then pinch each short end closed. Roll each rectangle into a rope about 9 inches long. Place ropes on baking sheets and form them into letters; if necessary (to make letters such as H, for example), cut ropes into pieces with butter knife and pinch ends of pieces closed. Space letters 2 inches apart. Let letters rise in a warm place for about 2 hours, until doubled in size.

3 About 20 minutes before letters are done rising, preheat oven to 375°.

4 Bake letters for about 10 minutes, until golden brown. Turn off oven and use mitts to remove baking sheets to racks; let letters cool slightly before serving.

Makes 12 servings.

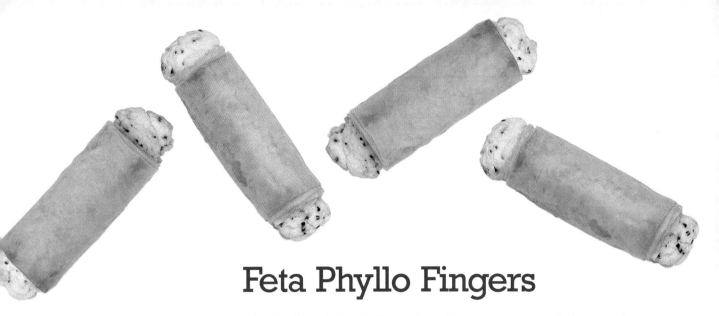

Feta Phyllo Fingers

INGREDIENTS

8 ounces feta cheese

1 cup (about 8 oz.) nonfat or lowfat cottage cheese

2 eggs

1 teaspoon dry oregano

¼ teaspoon pepper

2 tablespoons olive oil

8 sheets phyllo dough (*each* about 12 by 17 inches), thawed if frozen

EQUIPMENT

Measuring cups

Measuring spoons

Small bowl

Large bowl

12- by 15-inch baking sheet

Electric mixer

Butter knife

Pastry brush

Wire rack

Oven mitts

Plastic wrap

Phyllo dough is delicate, but fun to use—and the results are delicious! You can substitute mozzarella cheese for the feta cheese.

1 Preheat oven to 350°.

2 Crumble feta cheese into large bowl. Add cottage cheese, eggs, oregano, and pepper and beat with electric mixer until well blended.

3 Pour oil into small bowl. Lay one sheet of phyllo dough on a work surface (keep remaining dough covered airtight with plastic wrap). Use pastry brush to brush dough sheet lightly with oil. Place about ¼ cup of cheese mixture at center of one short end of dough sheet. Fold one long side lengthwise to cover cheese mixture; repeat with other long side. Starting at short filled end, roll up dough into a cylinder. Place phyllo roll on baking sheet and cover with plastic wrap.

4 Repeat step 3 to fill and shape remaining phyllo dough sheets, placing phyllo rolls about 1 inch apart on baking sheet. When all phyllo has been shaped, remove plastic wrap from baking sheet. Bake for about 25 minutes, until rolls are golden brown. Turn off oven and use mitts to remove baking sheet to rack. Let cool slightly before serving.

Makes 8 servings.

Lemon-Zucchini Loaf

Cut big slices of this moist bread to share with friends; see if they can guess what the green bits are. The recipe makes two loaves, so you can store one for another day.

INGREDIENTS

Margarine or butter to grease loaf pans

All-purpose flour to flour loaf pans

1 pound (about 4) small zucchini

2 lemons

3 cups all-purpose flour

1 tablespoon baking powder

1 cup walnut pieces

1 cup salad oil

2 cups sugar

3 eggs

EQUIPMENT

Measuring cups

Measuring spoons

Medium-size bowl

Large bowl

Two 5- by 9-inch loaf pans

Electric mixer

Butter knife

Utility knife

Utility spoon

Rubber spatula

Grater (or food processor for grating zucchini)

Juicer

Wooden pick

Cutting board

Wire rack

Oven mitts

Wax paper

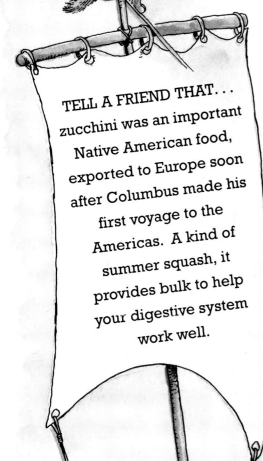

TELL A FRIEND THAT...
zucchini was an important Native American food, exported to Europe soon after Columbus made his first voyage to the Americas. A kind of summer squash, it provides bulk to help your digestive system work well.

1 Preheat oven to 350°. Lightly grease and flour loaf pans.

2 Rinse zucchini, but do not peel them. Use utility knife to cut off ends of zucchini on cutting board. Use large holes of grater to grate zucchini carefully onto wax paper (or grate with food processor).

3 Use small holes of grater to carefully grate enough peel from lemons to make 2 tablespoons (grate off only the colored part of peel). Use utility knife to cut lemons in half crosswise on cutting board; use juicer to squeeze ¼ cup juice from lemons.

4 Place 3 cups flour, baking powder, and walnut pieces in medium-size bowl and mix with utility spoon until well blended.

5 Place oil, sugar, lemon peel, and lemon juice in large bowl and beat with electric mixer until blended. Add eggs, one at a time, and beat after each addition until well blended.

6 Add flour mixture to egg mixture and mix with spoon until blended. Add zucchini and mix with spoon until well blended. Pour batter equally into loaf pans, scraping out bowl with spatula. Bake for about 50 minutes, until wooden pick inserted in center of each loaf comes out clean. Turn off oven and use mitts to remove pans to rack. Let loaves cool in pans for 10 minutes. Use mitts to tilt pans so loaves tip out onto rack; turn loaves right side up and let cool.

Makes 2 loaves (8 servings per loaf).

No-nonsense Nachos

Make your own tortilla chips to dip into spicy black beans, melted jack cheese, and your favorite mild or hot salsa.

INGREDIENTS

1 package (10 to 12 oz.) corn tortillas (about 6-inch diameter)

2 cans (about 15 oz. *each*) black beans

1 teaspoon chili powder

½ cup bottled salsa

1 cup (4 oz.) shredded jack cheese

EQUIPMENT

Measuring cups

Measuring spoons

Medium-size bowl

9-inch pie pan

Two 10- by 15-inch baking pans

Butter knife

Utility knife

Utility spoon

Pancake turner

Potato masher

Can opener

Colander

Cutting board

Wire racks

Oven mitts

Heatproof serving plate

TELL A FRIEND THAT...
black beans are a variety of legume
native to Mexico; they're especially
popular in Central and South America.
Black beans are rich in protein (important
for fighting infection) and in a type of fiber
that helps keep your heart healthy.

1 Preheat oven to 500°.

2 Half-fill bowl with water. Dip tortillas, one at a time, into water; shake off extra water and stack tortillas on cutting board. Use utility knife to cut stack of tortillas into 6 pie-shaped wedges. Spread tortilla pieces out in a single layer in baking pans. Bake for 3 minutes; then use mitts to remove pans carefully to racks. Use pancake turner to turn tortilla pieces over and use mitts to return pans to oven. Bake for about 2 more minutes, until chips are light golden. Use mitts to remove pans carefully to racks. Reduce oven temperature to 400°.

3 Place beans in colander and rinse with water until water runs clear.

4 Wash and dry bowl. Place beans and chili powder in bowl and mash with potato masher until well blended. Use utility spoon to spread bean mixture in pie pan; cover with salsa and top with cheese. Bake for about 25 minutes, until cheese is golden brown. Turn off oven and use mitts to remove pan to rack. To serve, place pie pan on serving plate and surround with chips.

Makes 6 servings.

Dawn-to-Dusk Granola

Sweetened with a generous helping of honey, this blend of fruit, nuts, and grains is worth trying any time of day. You may use your favorite dried fruit in place of the mixed fruit bits.

INGREDIENTS

1 large navel orange

4 cups regular rolled oats

1 cup wheat germ

½ cup pecan pieces

½ cup sliced almonds

¼ cup salad oil

½ cup honey

½ teaspoon vanilla

1 package (6 oz.) dried mixed fruit bits

EQUIPMENT

Measuring cups

Measuring spoons

Large bowl

10- by 15-inch baking pan

Butter knife

Wooden spoon

Grater

Wire rack

Oven mitts

Wax paper

2-quart airtight storage container

 Preheat oven to 325°.

2 Use small holes of grater to carefully grate peel of orange onto wax paper (grate off only the colored part of peel).

3 Place orange peel, oats, wheat germ, pecan pieces, and sliced almonds in bowl and mix with wooden spoon until well blended. Add oil, honey, and vanilla and mix with spoon until well blended.

4 Spread granola in baking pan and bake for 15 minutes. Use mitts to remove pan to rack; stir granola with spoon and use mitts to return pan to oven. Bake for about 15 more minutes, until almonds are golden brown. Turn off oven and use mitts to remove pan to rack. Let granola cool, stirring occasionally. When granola is completely cool, stir in dried fruit bits. Then pour granola into storage container and store in refrigerator.

Makes 8 cups (about 32 servings).

Quick Fruit Dip

Stick wooden picks into grapes, pineapple chunks, and tangerine or mandarin orange sections; then dip them in this sweet, spicy blend of applesauce and yogurt.

INGREDIENTS

1 cup unsweetened applesauce

1 cup nonfat or lowfat vanilla yogurt

1 teaspoon ground cinnamon

¼ teaspoon ground nutmeg

EQUIPMENT

Measuring cups

Measuring spoons

Medium-size bowl

Butter knife

Utility spoon

1 Place applesauce, yogurt, cinnamon, and nutmeg in bowl and mix with utility spoon until well blended.

Makes 2 cups (about 16 servings).

Quick Vegetable Dip

Just two ingredients go into this creamy herb dip. Serve it as a dunk for cherry tomatoes, baby carrots, and radishes.

INGREDIENTS

1 package (4 oz.) reduced-fat garlic and herb cheese spread

1 cup light sour cream

EQUIPMENT

Measuring cups

Medium-size bowl

Utility spoon

1 Place cheese spread and sour cream in bowl and mix with utility spoon until well blended.

Makes 1⅓ cups (about 10 servings).

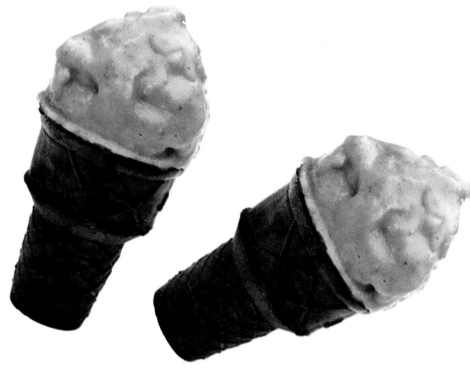

Frozen Fruit Cones

Create your own strawberry frozen yogurt and serve it in brightly colored ice cream cones.

INGREDIENTS

⅔ cup fresh strawberries; or ⅔ cup frozen unsweetened whole strawberries, thawed

¼ cup sugar

1⅓ cups nonfat plain yogurt

4 ice cream cones

EQUIPMENT

Measuring cups

9- by 13-inch baking pan

Blender or food processor

Butter knife

Utility spoon

Plastic wrap or foil

1 If you are using fresh strawberries, pull off leaves. Then place fresh or frozen strawberries, sugar, and yogurt in blender; cover and whirl until smooth. Pour into baking pan, cover with plastic wrap, and freeze for about 2 hours, until firm. Use utility spoon to scoop frozen yogurt into ice cream cones.

Makes 4 servings.

TELL A FRIEND THAT. . . yogurt is made by adding bacterial cultures to milk. It's an excellent source of calcium, essential for maintaining strong bones.

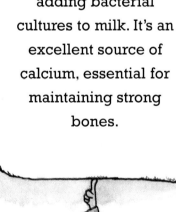

Really Raspberry Shake

Share this quick-to-fix milkshake with friends who love raspberries. You may use fresh or frozen fruit.

INGREDIENTS

2 cups fresh raspberries; or 2 cups frozen raspberries, thawed

1 cup nonfat or lowfat milk

1 cup raspberry frozen yogurt

EQUIPMENT

Measuring cups

Blender

1 Place raspberries, milk, and yogurt in blender. Cover and whirl until smooth.

Makes 4 servings.

Make Your Own Soda

You can create a variety of sodas by changing the frozen fruit juice you use as the base. How about apple in place of grape juice?

INGREDIENTS

1 can (12 oz.) frozen grape juice

4½ cups sparkling water

EQUIPMENT

Measuring cups

Half-gallon pitcher

Utility spoon

1 Place juice in pitcher, add sparkling water, and mix with utility spoon until well blended.

Makes 6 servings.

MENU

SNACK BAR

CASH BOX

At the Movies

Set up a snack bar that will have customers coming back for more.

- Prepare Dawn-to-Dusk Granola and frozen yogurt for Frozen Fruit Cones.

- Make signs for each snack; include each item's price.

- Make paper money, using a different color for amounts from 1¢ to $1.

- Make a cash register out of a tissue box, cutting off half the top.

- Set up a table for the snacks, signs, and cash register. Find a pencil and paper.

- Prepare No-nonsense Nachos and Make Your Own Soda. Assemble Frozen Fruit Cones.

- Place the snacks, signs, cash register, pencil, and paper on the table.

- Hand out money to your friends and place some in the register.

- Let your friends buy whatever they want at your snack bar. Use your pencil and paper to figure out correct change.

- Take turns playing charades, acting out the titles of your favorite movies, while you eat your snacks.

- Don't forget to take a break for more refreshments.

DOUBLY DAZZLING DESSERTS

Double-dipped Strawberries

Strawberries dipped in white and dark chocolate are perfect for parties—and really easy to make.

1 Cover baking sheet with wax paper. Place strawberries (do not remove leaves) in colander and rinse gently with cool water. Drain berries completely on paper towels and pat dry.

INGREDIENTS

32 strawberries

12 ounces white chocolate

1½ teaspoons vegetable shortening

6 ounces semisweet chocolate

EQUIPMENT

Measuring spoons

Double boiler

12- by 15-inch baking sheet

Butter knife

Whisk

Colander

Paper towels

Wax paper

2 Place white chocolate and 1 teaspoon of the shortening in top of double boiler. Pour water into bottom of double boiler, being sure water will not touch bottom of top pan. Place bottom of double boiler on burner and bring water to a boil over high heat. Turn off burner, put top of double boiler in place over hot water, cover, and let stand for about 5 minutes, until chocolate is melted. Uncover and mix chocolate and shortening with whisk until well blended.

3 Holding berries by the leaves, dip about three-fourths of each berry into white chocolate; place berries on wax paper.

4 Wash and thoroughly dry top of double boiler and repeat step 2, using semisweet chocolate and remaining ½ teaspoon shortening. Holding same berries by the leaves, dip about half of each berry into semisweet chocolate. Place on wax paper and let stand for at least 15 minutes or up to 4 hours before serving.

Makes 32 double-dipped strawberries.

Crushed Pineapple Cream

Pick a pretty mold to show off this cool and refreshing dessert. Pineapple yogurt adds rich, creamy flavor.

INGREDIENTS

½ cup sugar

1 envelope unflavored gelatin

½ cup water

1 cup light sour cream

2 cups lowfat pineapple yogurt

1 small can (about 8 oz.) crushed pineapple packed in its own juice

EQUIPMENT

Measuring cups

Medium-size bowl

4- to 5-cup mold

1- to 1½-quart pan

Butter knife

Utility spoon

Whisk

Can opener

Colander

Wire rack

Plastic wrap or foil

Towel

Serving plate

1 Place sugar and gelatin in pan and mix with whisk until blended; add water and let stand for 5 minutes to soften gelatin. Place pan on burner and bring gelatin mixture to a boil over medium-high heat, stirring with whisk. Turn off burner and remove pan to rack.

2 Place sour cream, yogurt, and gelatin mixture in bowl and mix with whisk until well blended. Cover with plastic wrap and refrigerate for about 1 hour, until partially set. Meanwhile, place pineapple in colander and let drain. Add pineapple to partially set yogurt mixture and mix with utility spoon until well blended. Pour into mold, cover with plastic wrap, and refrigerate until set (about 5 hours) or until next day.

3 To unmold, fill sink about half full of hot-to-touch water. Dip mold up to its rim in water for a few seconds, just until edges of dessert begin to melt. Quickly lift out mold and dry with towel; then place serving plate upside down on top of mold. Holding plate and mold together, turn both over; let stand briefly to let dessert slip free, then lift off mold.

Makes 8 servings.

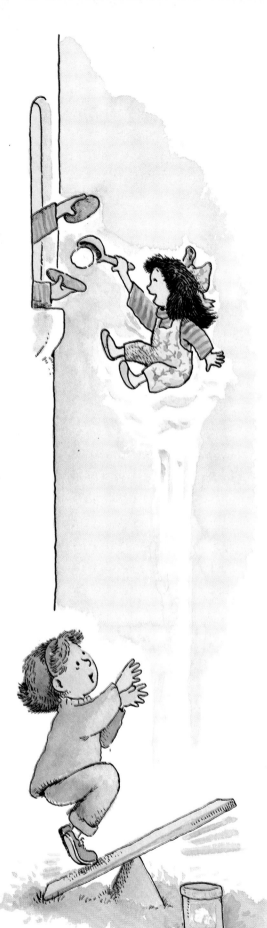

Gingersnap Sandwiches

Sandwich vanilla frozen yogurt (or another flavor, if you like) between spicy ginger cookies.

INGREDIENTS

Margarine or butter to grease baking sheets

2 cups all-purpose flour

2 teaspoons baking soda

¼ teaspoon salt

1 teaspoon ground ginger

1 teaspoon ground cinnamon

1 teaspoon ground cloves

¾ cup margarine or butter, at room temperature

1¼ cups sugar

¼ cup light molasses

1 egg

1 quart vanilla frozen yogurt

EQUIPMENT

Measuring cups

Measuring spoons

Medium-size bowl

Large bowl

Small dish

Three 12- by 15-inch baking sheets

Electric mixer

Butter knife

Utility spoon

Pancake turner

Ruler

Wire racks

Oven mitts

1 Preheat oven to 350°. Lightly grease baking sheets.

2 Place flour, baking soda, salt, ginger, cinnamon, and cloves in medium-size bowl and mix with utility spoon until well blended.

3 Place ¾ cup margarine and 1 cup of the sugar in large bowl and beat with electric mixer until blended. Add molasses and egg and beat until blended. Add flour mixture to egg mixture and beat until well blended.

4 Roll dough into about 1½-inch balls with your hands (you should have 32 balls). Place remaining ¼ cup sugar in

small dish and roll balls in sugar. Place balls on baking sheets, spacing them about 3 inches apart. Bake for about 10 minutes, until cookies are golden. Turn off oven and use mitts to remove baking sheets to racks. Let cookies cool on baking sheets for about 5 minutes; then use pancake turner to transfer cookies to racks. Let cool completely.

5 For each sandwich, spoon ¼ cup frozen yogurt on bottom side of one cookie; press another cookie, bottom side down, over yogurt.

Makes 16 sandwiches (16 servings).

Pass the Peanut Butter Cookies

You won't want to stop at just one of these chewy, nutty cookies—but if you do have any extras, store them in an airtight container.

INGREDIENTS

Margarine or butter to grease baking sheets

1 cup whole wheat flour

1 teaspoon baking soda

2 cups regular rolled oats

½ cup margarine or butter, at room temperature

1 cup old-fashioned chunky peanut butter

1 cup granulated sugar

½ cup firmly packed brown sugar

2 eggs

½ cup nonfat or lowfat milk

EQUIPMENT

Measuring cups

Measuring spoons

Medium-size bowl

Large bowl

Three 12- by 15-inch baking sheets

Electric mixer

Butter knife

Utility spoon

Pancake turner

Ruler

Wire racks

Oven mitts

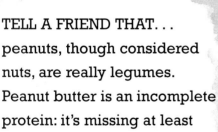

TELL A FRIEND THAT...
peanuts, though considered nuts, are really legumes. Peanut butter is an incomplete protein: it's missing at least one of the essential amino acids. For maximum health benefits, it should be eaten in combination with grains or complete protein.

1 Preheat oven to 350°. Lightly grease baking sheets.

2 Place flour, baking soda, and oats in medium-size bowl and mix with utility spoon until well blended.

3 Place ½ cup margarine, peanut butter, granulated sugar, and brown sugar in large bowl and beat with electric mixer until blended. Add eggs and beat until blended. Add milk and flour mixture and beat until well blended.

4 Drop dough by rounded tablespoons onto baking sheets, spacing cookies about 2 inches apart. Bake for about 12 minutes, until edges of cookies are lightly browned. Turn off oven and use mitts to remove baking sheets to racks. Let cookies cool on baking sheets for about 5 minutes; then use pancake turner to transfer cookies to racks.

Makes about 36 cookies.

No-problem Pie

The pat-in crust makes this pie especially easy to prepare. It's fun to pit fresh cherries, but you may also use frozen pitted fruit.

INGREDIENTS

1 cup all-purpose flour

½ cup plus 2 tablespoons sugar

½ cup margarine or butter

2 eggs

6 cups fresh Bing cherries or frozen pitted dark sweet cherries

1 lemon

¼ teaspoon almond extract

3 tablespoons cornstarch

EQUIPMENT

Measuring cups

Measuring spoons

Large bowl

9-inch pie pan

10- by 15-inch baking pan

Food processor or medium-size bowl

Butter knife

Utility knife

Utility spoon

Rubber spatula

Cherry pitter

Juicer

Cutting board

Wire rack

Oven mitts

Foil

TELL A FRIEND THAT... wild cherries are native to North America, but the first domestic types were brought from Europe by the colonists. A source of vitamin A, cherries can help keep your hair and skin healthy.

1 Place oven rack on lowest level of oven. Preheat oven to 400°. Line 10- by 15-inch baking pan with foil.

2 Place flour and 2 tablespoons of the sugar in food processor; cover and whirl until blended. (Or place in medium-size bowl and mix with utility spoon until blended.) Use butter knife to cut margarine into chunks on cutting board. Add margarine to flour mixture and whirl until mixture looks like coarse meal (or rub margarine into flour with your fingers). Separate each egg and reserve whites for another use; add egg yolks to flour mixture and whirl (or mix with spoon) until dough holds together. Press dough evenly over bottom and up sides of pie pan with your hands.

3 If you are using fresh cherries, pit them with cherry pitter. Place fresh or frozen pitted cherries in large bowl. Use utility knife to cut lemon in half crosswise on cutting board; use juicer to squeeze 1 tablespoon juice from lemon. Add lemon juice, almond extract, remaining ½ cup sugar, and cornstarch to cherries and mix with utility spoon until well blended. Set pie pan in foil-lined baking pan. Spoon cherry mixture into crust, scraping out bowl with spatula. Bake for about 55 minutes, until crust is golden brown and filling is bubbly. Turn off oven and use mitts to remove pan carefully to rack. Let pie cool for about 30 minutes. Serve warm or at room temperature.

Makes 8 servings.

Ooey Gooey Brownie Cake

Brownies or cake? You can have both when you frost this fudgy concoction with a dark chocolate icing.

INGREDIENTS

Margarine or butter to grease baking pan

All-purpose flour to flour baking pan

2½ cups all-purpose flour

1 teaspoon baking soda

½ teaspoon salt

1¼ cups margarine or butter, at room temperature

2 cups (12 oz.) semisweet chocolate chips

2 cups granulated sugar

4 eggs

2½ teaspoons vanilla

1 cup powdered sugar

1 tablespoon nonfat or lowfat milk

EQUIPMENT

Measuring cups

Measuring spoons

Medium-size bowl

2-quart pan

3-quart pan

9- by 13-inch baking pan

Butter knife

Utility spoon

Whisk

Rubber spatula

Wire rack

Oven mitts

1 Preheat oven to 350°. Lightly grease and flour baking pan.

2 Place 2½ cups flour, baking soda, and salt in bowl and mix with utility spoon until well blended.

3 Place 3-quart pan on burner; add 1 cup of the margarine and 1¾ cups of the chocolate chips. Melt over low heat, stirring with whisk until blended. Turn off burner and add granulated sugar, eggs, and 2 teaspoons of the vanilla; mix with whisk until well blended. Add flour mixture to chocolate mixture and mix with spoon until well blended. Spoon into baking pan,

scraping out bowl with spatula. Bake for 35 minutes. Turn off oven and use mitts to remove pan to rack (cake will fall slightly in center).

4 Wash and dry whisk and spatula. Place 2-quart pan on burner; add remaining ¼ cup margarine and remaining ¼ cup chocolate chips. Melt over low heat, stirring with whisk until blended. Turn off burner. Add powdered sugar, milk, and remaining ½ teaspoon vanilla; mix with whisk until well blended. Pour frosting over warm cake and spread evenly with spatula. Let cool in pan.

Makes 24 servings.

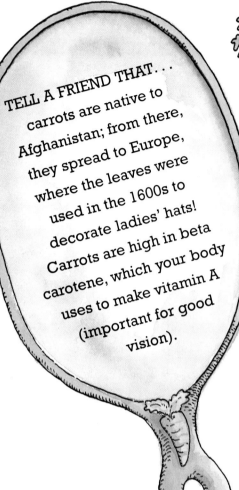
Ultimate Carrot Cake

Planning a big celebration? You can feed a crowd with this moist spice cake covered with rich, creamy frosting.

INGREDIENTS

Margarine or butter to grease baking pan

All-purpose flour to flour baking pan

1 pound carrots

2½ cups whole wheat flour

2 teaspoons baking powder

1 teaspoon baking soda

1½ teaspoons ground cinnamon

1 teaspoon ground nutmeg

½ teaspoon ground cloves

1 cup salad oil

1½ cups granulated sugar

4 eggs

½ cup buttermilk

6 ounces Neufchâtel cheese, at room temperature

1 box (1 lb.) powdered sugar

1 teaspoon vanilla

1 tablespoon nonfat or lowfat milk

EQUIPMENT

Measuring cups

Measuring spoons

Medium-size bowl

Large bowl

9- by 13-inch baking pan

Electric mixer

Butter knife

Utility spoon

Rubber spatula

Grater or food processor

Vegetable peeler

Wooden pick

Wire rack

Oven mitts

Wax paper

1 Preheat oven to 350°. Lightly grease and flour baking pan.

2 Peel carrots and use large holes of grater to grate carrots carefully onto wax paper (or grate with food processor).

3 Place whole wheat flour, baking powder, baking soda, cinnamon, nutmeg, and cloves in medium-size bowl and mix with utility spoon until well blended.

4 Place oil and granulated sugar in large bowl and beat with electric mixer until well blended. Add eggs, one at a time, and beat until well blended after each addition.

5 Add flour mixture and buttermilk to egg mixture and beat on low speed until blended. Add carrots and mix with spoon until well blended. Pour batter into pan, scraping out bowl with spatula. Bake for about 45 minutes, until wooden pick inserted in center of cake comes out clean. Turn off oven and use mitts to remove pan to rack; let cake cool completely.

6 Wash and dry large bowl and electric mixer beaters. Place Neufchâtel cheese, powdered sugar, vanilla, and milk in bowl and beat until well blended. Use butter knife to spread frosting on cooled cake.

Makes 18 servings.

MENU

NO SITTING

Everything's Backwards

This is a special and especially silly family dinner.

- Write invitations on colored paper that say:

  You are invited to an "Everything's Backwards Party" tonight. Please R.S.V.P. by signing the following and returning it to me:

  > I promise to eat my dinner from finish to start,
  > signed _____.

  P.S. Please wear one piece of clothing backwards.

- Make place cards by writing names backwards on bottoms of slips of paper; fold papers lengthwise to stand up on the table.

- Prepare No-problem Pie and Quick Vegetable Dip. Set pie aside and refrigerate dip.

- Set the table, mixing up the positions of the utensils.

- Prepare Windy Weather Stew. When stew is done, turn oven to 175°. Leave stew in oven. Prepare Simply Steamed Broccoli. Let broccoli stand in pan while you eat dessert.

- While you enjoy your meal, share a favorite fairy tale, telling it from "And they lived happily ever after..." to "Once upon a time...".

- !nuf evaH

HAPPY HOLIDAYS & SPECIAL OCCASIONS

Chinese New Year
Barbecued Spareribs

Forget the coals—you "barbecue" these ribs in the oven. You can marinate the meat the day before you bake it.

INGREDIENTS

¾ cup sugar

½ cup reduced-sodium soy sauce

¼ cup hoisin sauce

¼ cup reduced-sodium chicken broth

1 teaspoon ground ginger

1 rack pork spareribs (3 to 4 lbs.); have the meatman saw the ribs in half crosswise

EQUIPMENT

Measuring cups

Measuring spoons

Two 12- by 17-inch baking pans

Butter knife

Utility knife

Fork

Utility spoon

Can opener

Cutting board

Wire rack

Oven mitts

Foil

1 Place sugar, soy sauce, hoisin sauce, chicken broth, and ginger in one baking pan and mix with utility spoon until well blended. Lay ribs in pan and use spoon to coat ribs with soy mixture. Cover with foil and refrigerate, turning ribs over occasionally, for at least 4 hours or until next day.

2 Preheat oven to 350°. Line second baking pan with foil. Lift ribs from soy mixture and place them in foil-lined pan (discard any remaining soy mixture). Bake ribs for 1 hour, until meat is browned; use mitts to remove pan to rack. Use fork to remove ribs to cutting board; use utility knife to cut meat to bone. If meat is still pink, return to pan with fork. Use mitts to return pan to oven; bake for about 15 more minutes, then repeat test. When meat is no longer pink, turn off oven. Use utility knife to cut between rib bones to serve.

Makes 6 servings.

Valentine's Day
Sweetheart Cake

Some simple cutting and shaping change a square and circle into a heart. If you don't have a large round serving tray, you can make an attractive tray by covering a baking sheet with foil.

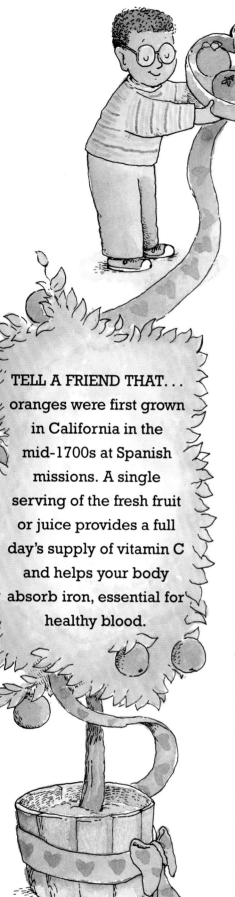

TELL A FRIEND THAT... oranges were first grown in California in the mid-1700s at Spanish missions. A single serving of the fresh fruit or juice provides a full day's supply of vitamin C and helps your body absorb iron, essential for healthy blood.

INGREDIENTS

Butter to grease baking pans

Cake flour to flour baking pans

3 cups cake flour

1 tablespoon baking powder

½ teaspoon salt

¼ teaspoon baking soda

1¾ cups granulated sugar

1¼ cups butter, at room temperature

2 eggs

¾ cup nonfat or lowfat milk

1 cup orange juice

1 box (1 lb.) powdered sugar

Red and pink colored sugar, if you like

EQUIPMENT

Measuring cups

Measuring spoons

Medium-size bowl

Large bowl

9-inch-round baking pan

9-inch-square baking pan

Electric mixer

Butter knife

Utility spoon

Rubber spatula

Wooden pick

Cutting board

Wire rack

Oven mitts

19-inch-round serving tray.

1 Preheat oven to 350°. Lightly grease and flour round and square baking pans.

2 Place 3 cups flour, baking powder, salt, and baking soda in medium-size bowl and mix with utility spoon until well blended.

3 Place granulated sugar and ¾ cup of the butter in large bowl and beat with electric mixer until well blended. Add eggs, one at a time, and beat until well blended after each addition. Add half the flour mixture, the milk, and ¾ cup of the orange juice and mix on low speed until blended; add remaining flour mixture and mix on low speed until blended. Pour batter into pans (put slightly more batter in square pan than in round), scraping out bowl with spatula. Bake for about 30 minutes, until wooden pick inserted in center of each cake comes out clean. Turn off oven and use mitts to remove pans to rack. Let cakes cool in pans for 10 minutes. Remove cakes from pans; turn cakes right side up and let them cool completely.

4 Wash and dry large bowl. Place powdered sugar, remaining ½ cup butter, and remaining ¼ cup orange juice in bowl and beat with electric mixer on low speed until frosting is light and fluffy.

5 Use butter knife to cut round cake in half on cutting board to make 2 semicircles. Place square cake on serving tray with one pointed corner at bottom of tray. Place a semicircle on each of the top sides of the square to form a heart shape. Use butter knife to spread frosting on cake. Decorate with colored sugar, if you like.

Makes 16 to 20 servings.

Cinco de Mayo
Chicken & Tortilla Casserole

Invite company over to share this holiday entrée of creamy chicken, corn tortillas, and green salsa.

INGREDIENTS

6 skinless, boneless chicken breast halves

1 jar (about 1 lb.) salsa verde

1 cup light sour cream

½ cup half-and-half

12 corn tortillas (about 6-inch diameter)

4 cups (1 lb.) shredded Cheddar cheese

⅓ cup grated Parmesan cheese

EQUIPMENT

Measuring cups

Small bowl

4- to 5-quart pan & lid

9- by 13-inch baking pan

Butter knife

Utility knife

Utility spoon

Slotted spoon

Ruler

Cutting board

Wire rack

Oven mitts

Foil

1 Rinse chicken with cold water. Place 4- to 5-quart pan on burner. Half-fill pan with water; bring water to a boil over high heat. Turn off burner, carefully add chicken, and cover. Let chicken stand in water for 20 minutes. Uncover pan and use slotted spoon to lift one piece of chicken to cutting board. Cut chicken to center of thickest part with utility knife. If chicken is still pink inside, return it to pan, cover, and let stand for 10 more minutes; then repeat test. When chicken is no longer pink, remove all chicken with slotted spoon to board. Cut into bite-size pieces with utility knife.

2 Preheat oven to 350°.

3 Place half the chicken in baking pan and use utility spoon to cover chicken with half the salsa. Place sour cream and half-and-half in bowl and mix with spoon until well blended. Spoon half the mixture over salsa.

4 Use utility knife to cut tortillas into ¼-inch-wide strips on cutting board. Top sour cream mixture with half the tortilla strips and half the Cheddar cheese. Repeat layers, using remaining chicken, salsa, sour cream mixture, tortilla strips, and Cheddar cheese.

5 Cover pan with foil and fold foil around pan edges to seal. Bake for 40 minutes. Use mitts to remove pan to rack. Carefully remove foil, starting at a side away from you to avoid steam; sprinkle top of casserole with Parmesan cheese. Use mitts to return pan to oven. Bake, uncovered, for about 5 minutes, until cheese is golden. Turn off oven and use mitts to remove pan to rack. Let stand for 10 minutes before serving.

Makes 8 servings.

TELL A FRIEND THAT... chicken was served at Greek and Roman feasts nearly 2,000 years ago. Chicken is rich in protein, iron, and B vitamins, all important for a healthy, energetic body.

Fourth of July
Pesto & Vegetable Couscous Salad

Mix brightly colored vegetables, couscous, and a basil-sparked sauce together—and you have the perfect salad for an Independence Day picnic.

INGREDIENTS

8 ounces broccoli, steamed as directed for Simply Steamed Veggies (page 55)

1½ cups water

1 cup couscous

1 cup fresh basil leaves

⅓ cup olive oil

1 clove garlic

½ teaspoon salt

¼ cup grated Parmesan cheese

8 ounces summer squash

8 ounces cherry tomatoes

2 tablespoons pine nuts

EQUIPMENT

Measuring cups

Measuring spoons

3-quart pan & lid

Food processor

Butter knife

Utility knife

Fork

Wooden spoon

Rubber spatula

Cutting board

102

1 Place steamed broccoli on cutting board. Use utility knife to cut off flowerets; then use knife to cut stalks crosswise into thin slices.

2 Place pan on burner, add water, and bring to a boil over high heat. Add couscous and stir with wooden spoon. Cover, turn off burner, and let stand while you prepare pesto.

3 To prepare pesto, place basil leaves, oil, garlic, salt, and cheese in food processor. Cover and whirl until well blended. Pour pesto into couscous, scraping out processor with spatula. Stir pesto into couscous with fork.

4 Use utility knife to cut squash crosswise into thin slices on cutting board. Use knife to cut cherry tomatoes in half lengthwise on board. Add squash, cherry tomatoes, broccoli flowerets and stalks, and pine nuts to couscous and mix with wooden spoon until blended.

Makes 6 servings.

Halloween
Witches' Blood

This brew is guaranteed to warm your bones on a blustery trick-or-treat night.

INGREDIENTS

4 cups cranberry juice cocktail

2 cups orange juice

1 tablespoon sugar

12 whole cloves

1 cinnamon stick

EQUIPMENT

Measuring cups

Measuring spoons

3-quart pan

Butter knife

Wooden spoon

Slotted spoon

1 Place pan on burner. Add cranberry juice cocktail, orange juice, sugar, cloves, and cinnamon stick and bring to a boil over high heat, stirring occasionally with wooden spoon. Reduce heat to low and simmer for 15 minutes. Remove cloves and cinnamon stick with slotted spoon.

Makes 6 servings.

TELL A FRIEND THAT...
apricots, grown in China thousands of years ago, were planted at Southern California missions in the 1700s. Apricots are an excellent source of vitamin A, which your nervous system needs to work properly.

Orange Worms

INGREDIENTS

2 cans (about 1 lb. *each*)
   apricot halves packed
   in light syrup

4 envelopes unflavored
   gelatin

2 cups orange juice

EQUIPMENT

Measuring cups

3-quart pan

9- by 13-inch baking pan

Food processor or blender

Butter knife

Whisk

Pancake turner

Can opener

Ruler

Colander

Wire rack

Plastic wrap or foil

Serving plate

See photograph on facing page. Wiggle these worms any way you want on your plate! If you like, give them "eyes" made from licorice bits.

1 Place apricots in colander and let drain. Place drained apricots in food processor, cover, and whirl until well blended.

2 Place gelatin in 3-quart pan, add orange juice, and let stand for 5 minutes to soften gelatin. Place pan on burner and bring to a boil over medium-high heat, stirring with whisk. Turn off burner and remove pan to rack. Add apricots and mix with whisk until well blended. Pour into baking pan, cover with plastic wrap, and refrigerate for about 4 hours, until set.

3 Use butter knife to cut gelatin crosswise into 9-inch-long, 1-inch-wide strips (you will have 13 strips). Use pancake turner to remove strips to serving plate; use your hands to twist strips into worm shapes.

Makes 13 servings.

Christmas & Hanukkah
Cut-out Cookies

Three ingredients and terrific! Choose cookie cutters to fit the occasion.

INGREDIENTS

1 cup butter, at room temperature

1 cup firmly packed brown sugar

2 cups all-purpose flour

Butter to grease baking sheets

All-purpose flour to flour work surface

Cake or cookie decorations, if you like

EQUIPMENT

Measuring cups

Large bowl

Four 12- by 15-inch baking sheets

Electric mixer

Butter knife

Pancake turner

Cookie cutters, about 2 inches in diameter

Ruler

Rolling pin

Wire racks

Oven mitts

Plastic wrap

106

1 Place 1 cup butter and brown sugar in bowl and beat with electric mixer until creamy. Slowly add 2 cups flour and beat on low speed until well blended. Gather dough into a ball with your hands, wrap in plastic wrap, and refrigerate until firm (about 1 hour) or for up to 3 days.

2 Preheat oven to 300°. Lightly grease baking sheets.

3 Lightly flour a work surface. Unwrap dough, place on surface, and use rolling pin to roll out to a thickness of ¼ inch. Cut out shapes with cookie cutters and use pancake turner to place cookies slightly apart on baking sheets. Top with decorations, if you like. Bake for about 15 minutes, until cookies are golden brown. Turn off oven and use mitts to remove baking sheets to racks. Use pancake turner to remove cookies from sheets to racks.

Makes about 48 cookies.

MENU

Stuffing-topped Pork Chops (page 52)

Apple Sweet Potatoes (page 53)

Simply Steamed Beans (page 55)

Sweetheart Cake (page 98)

Happy Anniversary!

Every day is the anniversary of something, so celebrate!

■ Decide why today is a special day to you: for example, it might be your second day with braces or your sixth day without braces.

■ Prepare Sweetheart Cake. Put the correct number of candles on the cake to mark the anniversary you are celebrating.

■ Make a sign announcing the reason, time, and place for the celebration dinner. Display it for everyone to see.

■ Make a poster of your cake; decorate it with one less than the number of candles you have put on the cake. Draw and cut out a paper candle for each dinner guest. Find a clean handkerchief and some tape.

■ Prepare Stuffing-topped Pork Chops, Apple Sweet Potatoes, and Simply Steamed Beans.

■ Enjoy your dinner. After dessert, use the handkerchief, tape, paper candles, and cake poster to play "Pin the candle on the cake."

Nutritional Analysis

On these pages, you'll find a nutritional analysis for each recipe in this book. The recipes are listed alphabetically by chapter.

Generally, the analysis applies to a single serving, based on the number of servings given for each recipe and the amount of each ingredient. If a range is given for the number of servings and/or the amount of an ingredient, the analysis is based on an average of the figures given.

The nutritional analysis does not include optional ingredients or those for which no specific amount is stated. If an ingredient is listed with a substitution, the information was calculated using the first choice.

Recipe	Calories	Fat (g)	Saturated Fat (g)	Carbohy-drates (g)	Protein (g)	Cholesterol (mg)	Sodium (mg)
BRIGHT-EYED BREAKFASTS							
All-in-one Oatmeal, p. 24	226	2	T	47	6	0	5
Allspice Baked Apples, p. 30	217	4	T	48	3	0	2
Berryful Muffins, p. 25	153	5	1	24	3	18	246
Cheddar Grits, p. 21	356	23	10	22	14	111	365
Garden Variety Omelet, p. 22	327	25	3	4	21	237	462
Ginger Peachy Coffeecake, p. 28	384	16	2	56	5	31	315
Lemon-Strawberry Waffles, p. 26	184	9	2	22	5	36	271
Mixed Berry Yogurt Topping, p. 31	56	2	T	9	2	0	10
Sausage Circles, p. 20	228	16	5	T	21	72	23
Too Two Smoothie, p. 31	108	T	T	27	1	0	2
LIP-SMACKING LUNCHES							
Already Ready Soup, p. 45	132	1	T	27	6	0	594
Can't Top It Pizza, p. 38	195	5	3	27	9	12	437
Fancy Fruit Salad, p. 42	191	7	1	30	6	1	47
Ham & Eggs Pie, p. 43	141	5	2	6	16	100	511
Lazy Day Chicken, p. 44	232	5	2	12	33	126	259
Made-ahead Meat Loaf, p. 46	506	21	7	54	24	90	807
Plenty of Potatoes, p. 47	266	8	2	41	6	8	132
Say Cheese & Smile Sandwiches, p. 37	396	22	6	44	12	17	335
Tuna-stuffed Pockets, p. 36	485	24	3	39	30	47	823
You're the Chef Salad, p. 40	574	39	9	31	30	58	622
DOWNRIGHT DELICIOUS DINNERS							
Apple Sweet Potatoes, p. 53	116	T	T	27	1	0	13
Colorful Swordfish Kebabs, p. 56	185	8	2	4	23	44	149
Corny Chili, p. 59	453	12	2	55	36	83	927
Layered Spinach Lasagne, p. 60	434	16	10	43	30	56	747

Recipe	Calories	Fat (g)	Saturated Fat (g)	Carbohy-drates (g)	Protein (g)	Cholesterol (mg)	Sodium (mg)
Ready Rice Pilaf, p. 57	141	1	T	28	4	0	323
Simply Steamed Beans, p. 55	31	T	T	7	2	0	6
Simply Steamed Broccoli, p. 55	25	T	T	5	3	0	24
Simply Steamed Carrots, p. 55	48	T	0	11	1	0	58
Speedy Shrimp Stir-fry, p. 58	146	1	T	19	16	111	525
Stuffing-topped Pork Chops, p. 52	272	10	3	16	30	73	575
Windy Weather Stew, p. 54	330	6	2	29	39	86	571
SUPER STAR SNACKS							
Alphabet Bread, p. 66	147	6	3	18	5	12	248
Dawn-to-Dusk Granola, p. 72	119	5	1	18	3	0	2
Feta Phyllo Fingers, p. 67	210	11	5	17	11	81	517
Frozen Fruit Cones, p. 74	143	10	T	20	6	2	86
Lemon-Zucchini Loaf, p. 68	374	20	3	46	5	40	100
Make Your Own Soda, p. 75	101	T	T	25	T	0	4
No-nonsense Nachos, p. 70	293	8	T	40	16	17	493
Quick Fruit Dip, p. 73	20	0	0	4	1	T	10
Quick Vegetable Dip, p. 73	65	5	2	2	2	15	46
Really Raspberry Shake, p. 75	97	1	T	18	4	5	57
DOUBLY DAZZLING DESSERTS							
Crushed Pineapple Cream, p. 81	176	5	2	30	5	12	34
Double-dipped Strawberries,* p. 80	90	5	1	10	1	2	9
Gingersnap Sandwiches, p. 82	269	10	2	40	4	16	278
No-problem Pie, p. 86	328	14	3	49	5	53	150
Ooey Gooey Brownie Cake, p. 88	307	15	2	41	4	36	204
Pass the Peanut Butter Cookies,* p. 84	134	7	1	16	3	12	98
Ultimate Carrot Cake, p. 90	384	16	3	57	5	55	164
HAPPY HOLIDAYS & SPECIAL OCCASIONS							
Barbecued Spareribs, p. 96	474	31	12	15	31	125	688
Chicken & Tortilla Casserole, p. 100	501	28	16	27	36	115	901
Cut-out Cookies,* p. 106	74	4	3	9	1	11	44
Orange Worms, p. 105	68	T	0	16	2	0	5
Pesto & Vegetable Couscous Salad, p. 102	285	15	3	32	8	3	263
Sweetheart Cake, p. 98	374	14	8	61	3	59	291
Witches' Blood, p. 104	143	T	T	36	1	0	5

T = less than .5
*Nutritional analysis given per piece

Index